PRAISE FOR
THE TRUTH ABOUT GETTING YOUR POINT ACROSS

"Success in life is about relationships, and healthy relationships are about communication. Pacelli helps us all take a leap forward in both with his new book, *The Truth about Getting Your Point Across*. I highly recommend it!"

—Chris Widener, president of Made for Success and author of **The Angel Inside**

"Everyone who aspires to effectively and successfully lead their organizations, large or small, public or private, should get this book and refer to it often. The points discussed are practical, immediately applicable, and will increase the effectiveness of any manager when applied."

—Luda Kopeikina, CEO of Noventra Corporation and author of **The Right Decision Every Time: How to Reach Perfect Clarity on Tough Decisions**

"*The Truth About Getting Your Point Across* works on several levels. First, it is a pragmatic guide to effective communication in virtually any setting. More important, these simple truths lay at the heart of effective leadership. I intend to keep this book on my desk as both a reference tool and a reminder of what it takes to be an effective leader."

—Bill Krippaehne, Managing Director of Norgate Online AS in Oslo, Norway, and former President and CEO of Fisher Communications, Inc., Seattle, WA

"Much of what is in this book I already know. But the demands of a busy life prevent me from communicating at my best. Pacelli fills this important gap by providing top-notch advice in a concise, organized format that can be accessed when I need it." I plan to keep his work handy and use it while in the trenches of day-to-day work."

—Clint Morse, CEO, The Mosaic Company

"There is an old saying that goes, 'There is nothing worse than the truth told at the wrong time.' When it comes to *The Truth About Getting Your Point Across*, it is just the opposite—these golden nuggets can mine opportunities for success and understanding. It's common sense and practical and should be required reading and on every CEO or leader's desk for constant review and understanding."

—Norman Rice, former Mayor of Seattle

"A solid, usable, practical guide to everyday business communications. Serious business professionals can put the ideas in the book to use immediately."

—John Patrick Dolan, Attorney at Law

"This book is a great resource—an easy reference guide and a useful tool that makes perfect sense. This down-to-earth and readable guide offers wise and practical examples of the wrong and right way to speak, to listen, and to hear. Every manager should keep a copy of Pacelli's *The Truth About Getting Your Point Across* at hand."

—Marilynn Sheldon, Managing Director,
The Fifth Avenue Theatre, Seattle, WA

"This is a fast, effective guide to persuading and convincing others in business and personal life. It really works."

—Brian Tracy, author of Goals!

THE TRUTH ABOUT GETTING YOUR POINT ACROSS

THE TRUTH ABOUT GETTING YOUR POINT ACROSS

...AND NOTHING BUT THE TRUTH

Lonnie Pacelli

An Imprint of Pearson Education
Upper Saddle River, NJ • New York • London • San Francisco • Toronto
Sydney • Tokyo • Singapore • Hong Kong • Cape Town • Madrid
Paris • Milan • Munich • Amsterdam

Vice President and Editor-in-Chief: Tim Moore
Acquisitions Editor: Paula Sinnott
Editorial Assistant: Susie Abraham
Development Editor: Russ Hall
Associate Editor-in-Chief and Director of Marketing: Amy Neidlinger
Cover Designer: Sandra Schroeder
Managing Editor: Gina Kanouse
Senior Project Editor: Lori Lyons
Copy Editor: Gayle Johnson
Senior Compositor: Gloria Schurick
Manufacturing Buyer: Dan Uhrig

© 2006 by Pearson Education, Inc.
Publishing as Prentice Hall
Upper Saddle River, New Jersey 07458

**Prentice Hall offers excellent discounts on this book when ordered in
quantity for bulk purchases or special sales. For more information,
please contact U.S. Corporate and Government Sales at 1-800-382-3419 or
corpsales@pearsontechgroup.com. For sales outside the U.S.,
please contact International Sales at 1-317-581-3793 or
international@pearsontechgroup.com.**

Printed in the United States of America

First Printing January 2006

ISBN 0-13-187371-7

Pearson Education LTD.
Pearson Education Australia PTY, Limited.
Pearson Education Singapore, Pte. Ltd.
Pearson Education North Asia, Ltd.
Pearson Education Canada, Ltd.
Pearson Educatión de Mexico, S.A. de C.V.
Pearson Education—Japan
Pearson Education Malaysia, Pte. Ltd.

Library of Congress Cataloging-in-Publication Data
Pacelli, Lonnie.
  The truth about getting your point across...and nothing but the truth / Lonnie Pacelli.
    p. cm.
  ISBN 0-13-187371-7
  1. Business communication. I. Title.
  HF5718.P33 2006
  658.4'5—dc22
                    2005017812

For ML, Boop, and GM.

CONTENTS

Contents

Contents

Contents

PREFACE

THE TRUTH ABOUT THIS BOOK

Wow, what a humbling challenge.

When I started working on *The Truth About Getting Your Point Across* with Prentice Hall, I did some serious soul-searching about how to approach the book to best relate to you, the busy reader who wants to get some good, practical advice quickly and then move on to the next item on your to-do list. I realized that, for this book to be most useful, it needed to be something you didn't just read once and then put on a shelf to forever gather dust. It needed to be something that was easy for you to pick up, get a few quick nuggets, and then apply them immediately. Because I wanted it to be personal, I've exposed my own failures (and a couple of successes) to help you avoid many of the perils and pitfalls I have encountered throughout my career. To that end, each of the truths in this book is written with the following in mind:

- **The truths are experience-based.** I've made tons of mistakes in over 20 years of attempting to get my point across in a myriad of situations. The stories, explanations, and advice you'll read are in large part based on things I have done *wrong* during my career. I've been whacked across the head with a 2-by-4 plenty of times when it comes to getting my point across and have learned many lessons the hard way.

My sincere hope is that you will be able to avoid many of the mistakes I've made, and this will help you get your point across more effectively.

- **The truths are situational.** I wanted to engineer a book that would be easy for you to read through once and then quickly refer to again and again depending on your particular situation, whether you are running a brainstorming session, developing a direction statement, or working with colleagues from another culture.

- **The truths are stand-alone.** I designed each truth so that it could stand on its own. This permits you to do more in-the-moment learning by quickly reading a truth, getting some practical advice, and then getting back to delivering results for your organization. Consequently, you may see advice duplicated in more than one truth. I thought it was important to paint a holistic picture in each truth to help you, the busy reader, be more effective.

- **The truths are practical.** Simply put, these truths work. Nothing fancy or heady—just direct and practical advice. Some truths buck conventional wisdom, and others reinforce things you may already know. I have learned (again, by doing things the wrong way) that many times we *know* the right thing to do, but we don't always *do* the right thing. If you start reading a truth and think, "Yeah, I know this," honestly say to yourself, "I *know* this, but do I *do* it?" Knowing something is great, but doing what you know delivers results.

You're busy, and I'm honored that you chose to take time out of your busy life to read what I have to say. I realize I owe you a rich and fulfilling experience that will help you get your point across more effectively in day-to-day situations. My sincere hope is that I have in some way helped you and have contributed to your success in whatever you do. Please feel free to e-mail me at point@leadingonedge.com and let me know what you think about *The Truth About Getting Your Point Across*.

To your effectiveness...

—Lonnie Pacelli

ACKNOWLEDGMENTS

First, thanks goes to the numerous managers, peers, and colleagues who helped mold and shape me throughout my career and who taught me great lessons in patience, humility, and empathy. The value I received was priceless.

Next, thanks to Paula Sinnott, acquisitions editor at Prentice Hall, for her tireless energy, enduring patience, and outstanding responsiveness in getting this book developed. Also thanks to Russ Hall, Louis Columbus, Sarah McArthur, David Leischner, Atul Tandon, Joe O'Konek, David Gill, Lou Pacelli, and Patricia Froelich for reviewing chapters and providing some outstanding feedback and counsel on how to make the book better. Also, a sincere thanks to the production team, led by Lori Lyons, and to Gayle Johnson for outstanding copyediting.

Special thanks to my wife and editor, Patty, for reading and rereading every chapter, providing clarity and conciseness to my words, and for being so responsive to my endless "Hey, can you read this?" requests. Also, thanks to my children, Briana and Trevor, for being the awesome kids they are and for helping me keep my priorities straight.

About the Author

Lonnie Pacelli is president of Leading on the Edge™ International and is the creator of Leading on the Edge™ Leadership Development Products and Services (www.leadingonedge.com). He has more than 20 years of management experience at both Microsoft and Accenture. During his 11 years at Accenture, he consulted with many Fortune 500 companies, including Motorola, Hughes Electronics, and Northrop-Grumman. During his nine years at Microsoft, he headed up development of some of Microsoft's internal systems, led its Corporate Procurement group, managed its Corporate Planning group, and led company-wide initiatives on continuous fiscal improvement and training process optimization.

He is also the author of *The Project Management Advisor: 18 Major Project Screw-Ups and How to Cut Them Off at the Pass* (www.projectmanagementadvisor.com). He is also a partner with Ascend Business Solutions, which focuses on consulting and back-office outsourcing for small businesses. Pacelli lives in Sammamish, Washington with his wife, Patty, and children Briana and Trevor. You can reach him at www.leadingonedge.com.

PART I

THE TRUTH ABOUT YOU AND YOUR RECIPIENT

TRUTH 1

GREAT COMMUNICATORS
CAN BE MADE

Ronald Reagan, the 40th president of the United States, was known as "the Great Communicator." He made one of his most famous statements during a speech at the Brandenburg Gate in West Berlin, Germany on June 12, 1987. During this speech, President Reagan threw down this challenge:

> *"General Secretary Gorbachev, if you seek peace, if you seek prosperity for the Soviet Union and Eastern Europe, if you seek liberalization: Come here to this gate! Mr. Gorbachev, open this gate! Mr. Gorbachev, tear down this wall!"*

Interestingly, the "tear down this wall" statement was vehemently opposed by foreign policy experts in Washington who had heavily lobbied the president not to say it. Ultimately, the lobbying was ignored, and Reagan included the challenge in his speech. On November 9, 1989, the border separating East Germany from West Germany was opened, and the wall came tumbling down. The Fall of The Wall will forever symbolize the end of the Cold War, which arguably was Reagan's greatest achievement as president.

Think back to some great communicators like Reagan, Martin Luther King, Jr., and John F. Kennedy. What made them great communicators? It wasn't that they were great orators, had flashy teeth, sported perfect hair, or demonstrated a flawless writing style. They had the following:

- **Courage.** They weren't afraid to speak out against the status quo and challenge conventional wisdom.
- **Conviction.** They felt strongly about their ideas and wanted others to know their viewpoint.
- **Wisdom.** They knew their subject matter cold and could defend their ideas effectively.
- **Clarity.** Their message was simple, concise, and easily understood.
- **Credibility.** They were trusted by others and walked the talk.

Courage. Conviction. Wisdom. Clarity. Credibility. Five attributes that are essential, regardless of whether you are speaking in front of hundreds of people, writing a report to your boss, or running a PTA meeting. Five attributes that build the foundation of someone who gets his or her point across effectively.

That someone can be you.

This book will help you better get your point across in a number of professional settings, including running meetings, delivering presentations, conducting interviews, and giving feedback. You'll get some very practical advice and helpful tips on being a more effective communicator. These tips combined with your courage, conviction, wisdom, clarity, and credibility can make you a great communicator who communicates great things and who knows how to get your point across in almost any setting.

Are you up for it?

TRUTH 2

SEEK TO UNDERSTAND YOUR RECIPIENT

From its earliest roots, communication has focused on sender and recipient having some common understanding of the information flowing between them. This means focusing not only on what you are broadcasting but also on what the other person is receiving. Too many times in business we default to thinking about communication from an outbound perspective (what we want to tell someone) instead of from an inbound perspective (what the recipient expects). I've seen plenty of reports, presentations, surveys, status reports, and just about any other type of communication go bust because the sender of the information didn't take the time to understand what the recipients were interested in, how they liked to receive information, and what was being asked of them.

In my career I have learned many lessons the hard way about understanding my recipient's communication preferences. Whether it was inappropriate drop-ins, written versus verbal communication, or raising issues to the wrong person, I've seemed to make just about every mistake you can make. After licking my wounds, I've learned to accept the mistakes as gems and understand how to better read my recipient when it comes to communication preferences.

Some of the most effective communicators I have worked with throughout my career were outstanding at understanding the following:

- Who needed to be communicated to
- What information they needed to help them do their job
- Why they needed information
- How they preferred to communicate
- How often they needed communication
- When they preferred communication to happen

Implementing and tailoring your communication method to your recipient can go a long way toward saving you countless hours of frustration and anxiety. For example, one of my favorite managers (and mentors) at Microsoft had a very distinct communication style:

- He liked to stay high-level and drill down into detail where he had questions.
- He liked to focus on areas where his input or decision was needed.
- He preferred verbal, face-to-face interaction versus e-mail.
- He did not like nonurgent, random phone calls or drop-ins.
- He liked to have biweekly one-on-one meetings and reserved time on his calendar to be available.
- He liked to know how I was thinking about solutions to my own problems versus my just dumping a problem on his doorstep.

When I started working for this manager, I quickly picked up on his communication style. Through subsequent interactions (and making a few mistakes), I adapted my style to his and zeroed in on the right communication approach. Throughout my duration with him, we had an outstanding working relationship, which all started with my understanding his communication idiosyncrasies and tailoring my style to meet his needs.

What if you don't know your recipient's preferences? Try some of these ideas:

- **Ask about her communication preferences.** Plan your questions, and set up a time to interview her on how she likes to communicate. Generally, people love to talk about themselves, and you'll likely get a lot of good information on how she likes to communicate.

- **Watch how she communicates.** Does she typically work with her door open or closed? Do others "drop in" for discussion? Does she keep a tight, structured calendar, or does she allow for flexibility? Does she like to stay on point during meetings, or is she open to some meandering in the conversation? Take a period of time—say, a week—and take good notes on how she interacts.

- **Ask others.** Coworkers or an administrative assistant might have some great insight into how your recipient likes to communicate. Get the scoop from someone else who has experience with the recipient.

Take a little time up front to understand the communication preferences of those you interact with on a regular basis. Be proactive about asking about preferences, observing communication styles, and getting coaching from others. You'll find that you will get more done in less time, you'll reduce your frustration level, and you'll ensure that your point gets across more effectively.

Take a little time to understand the communication preferences of those you interact with on a regular basis.

TRUTH 3

COMMUNICATION STYLES AREN'T
ONE-SIZE-FITS-ALL

Let's assume that you've taken the time to understand the recipient's communication expectations, as discussed in the preceding truth. Through your discovery process, you zero in on how the recipient likes to communicate. You discover, though, that his communication preferences are very different from your style of communicating. He may like structured appointments, while you may prefer "drop-ins." He might enjoy high-level reviews, where you tend toward more detailed discussions. He may prefer e-mail updates, while you function better with verbal updates. Yes, these are big differences, but this doesn't mean you'll forever be in a communication struggle. Quite frankly, you need to have a heart-to-heart discussion with yourself on what is more important: the content you are communicating or the mode in which you are communicating it.

Consider an example. Suppose you're attempting to get buy-off on a major project you're managing with your divisional vice president, and you have only 30 minutes to get your point across and get approval. You have a great project description document that has all the information necessary for justifying the project in a 40-page report. You have a couple of alternatives:

- Bring the project description report to the meeting, and walk through key report aspects with the divisional vice president.
- Prepare an executive summary PowerPoint-type document that presents key report aspects that are important to the divisional vice president.

With the first alternative, your preparation time for the meeting is minimal, because you have all the information prepared and ready to go. However, you run a significant risk of not getting your point across, because you have a lot of information and clutter that can get in the way. With the second alternative, your preparation time for the meeting is increased, because you are creating a special document that has information already contained in the charter document. However, your likelihood of getting your point across is increased, because you've taken away nonessential information and clutter that could get in the way.

This is a great time to ask yourself what is more important: getting approval for your project or saving yourself preparation time. On the surface, most people would say, "Duh—getting approval for the project!" Despite this viewpoint, I've been amazed at the number of times I've seen people in this very scenario choose the first alternative and go down in flames because the information was too clumsy to walk through. Getting approval for the project took second chair to an inappropriate mode of communicating the project. Ugly.

Also take note of this: However you adapt your communication style, make sure your passion doesn't get lost in the words. If your message has the passion of mashed potatoes, you'll have a more difficult time getting your point across effectively. So, regardless of how you adapt your communication style, do so with passion in your message.

Design your communication around your recipient.

The moral of the story is simple: design your communication around your recipient. It may mean that you have to adapt your style to meeting the situation and the recipient's preferences. It may mean that you "lose" because you're adapting to someone else versus their adapting to you. Put your ego aside and focus on the end, which is getting your point across, regardless of how you do it.

TRUTH 4

IF YOU THINK IT DOESN'T MAKE SENSE, IT PROBABLY DOESN'T

One of my managers was a bit inflexible when it came to communication. He was in many respects a very competent manager and knew his subject matter very well, but it was clear that I simply had to do things his way, or I got my head bitten off. One example of this was when I was managing a large project to reengineer some processes that employees use to enter customer orders for our products. We had prepared a large PowerPoint presentation for a number of key stakeholders to review some key design concepts. When I reviewed the presentation with my manager, he told me to create a Word document in addition to the PowerPoint document. The Word document would literally be a copy and paste from the PowerPoint document. When I asked why we needed a redundant document, the response was "Because this has to be in Word." I asked someone on the team to take everything we did in PowerPoint and copy and paste it into a Word document. We spent a significant amount of wasted time and money creating and maintaining a redundant document that no one read, all because one manager told me it had to be in Word.

Now, I'll admit I had a bad attitude about this and wasn't feeling very empathetic toward my manager, but I really struggled with the "It has to be in Word" answer.

Here's the million-dollar question: What is "realistic?" It depends on your point of view. What may be very realistic to me could be completely unrealistic to you. I've found it very helpful to look at three guidelines to find some common ground on reality:

- **Need.** In assessing need, you take a hard look at whether your recipient needs your information to do his or her job either now or in the future.

- **Frequency.** In looking at frequency, you assess how often you need to communicate to ensure that your recipient can act on your information in a timely manner.

- **Content depth.** With content depth, you determine how much information the recipient needs to do his or her job. For instance, the instruction manual on operating a cellular telephone does not need to explain how a signal travels to and from cellular towers to your cell phone.

Let's carry this forward to a simple scenario: A colleague has just started a new project that affects a small group of people within your department. She sends out very detailed daily e-mails to everyone in the department that communicate the project's status, what was accomplished the previous day, and what will be done the next day. The information, while very detailed, is largely redundant from day to day. She expects everyone in the department to read her daily status e-mails as the means of keeping up with the project.

What can make this communication unrealistic? Let's look at it using the three communication guidelines just mentioned:

- **Need.** Only the affected members in the department working directly with the project have a need for the information.
- **Frequency.** Getting information on a daily basis probably isn't necessary due to the redundancy of the information from day to day.
- **Content depth.** While some may benefit from very detailed information, it probably isn't necessary for the broader distribution.

To make the communications more realistic and applicable, the project manager should consider the following:

- Construct two separate communications—one for the small group of people who are directly affected by the project and a second communication for the rest of the department.
- For the small group directly affected by the project, gain specific agreement with them on need, frequency, and content depth of communications to ensure that they get what they need when they need it.
- For the rest of the department, look at ways in which other projects or organizations do broad-based communication, and mirror their frequency, content depth, and need. Look to department meetings, intranet websites, or other established communication vehicles for ideas.

Get aligned on your communication expectations. By gaining a common understanding of need, frequency, and content depth, you will go a long way toward ensuring clear communications between you and your recipient, and you will get your point across smoothly and effectively.

TRUTH 5

HELP OTHERS HELP THEMSELVES

Very early on in my career I did a presentation for some senior executives at a company I consulted for. In this presentation I did just about everything wrong. My slides had way too many words on them. I read the slides to the audience. I faced the screen too much instead of facing the audience. I didn't practice enough and confused even myself at one point. I mumbled instead of pronouncing my words clearly. In short, I was a disaster, and the client confirmed my poor performance by not awarding us the work.

After the presentation, my manager sat me down and gave me some very thoughtful, direct feedback on all the things I did wrong. I'd always admired his smooth, easygoing communication style and was very willing to listen. He offered some examples of presentations he had done and also left the door open for me to seek his advice and counsel on my communication style. His willingness to help me with my communication style affected me tremendously and imprinted upon me a desire to help my colleagues be more effective communicators.

Before I go any further, I want to reveal a basic philosophy I think is important about working with people. I want others to help me be better, and I want to help others be better. Through the years, this desire has at times been beneficial to me and my colleagues, and at other times it has gotten me into hot water because I didn't approach the situation appropriately. Having said that, I'd rather offer help to a colleague and let him or her choose to either take it or leave it as opposed to not offering help at all.

How do you go about helping your colleague be a better communicator? Consider using a few techniques:

- **Set the example.** In setting the example, you establish credibility with your colleague by demonstrating good communication skills through real-life experiences. Formal presentations, meeting facilitation, and written reports are great means by which you can help set an example and gain credibility as someone who can get his or her point across effectively. By setting the example, you teach through in-the-moment, real-time learning versus a more theoretical lab setting.

- **Openly share templates.** Do you have a great presentation format that has been effective in communicating with senior management? Or do you have an outstanding status reporting template that concisely shows a project's status? Freely make those templates available to others so that they can benefit from your work and maybe improve on your ideas.

■ **Make yourself available and open for advice and open to feedback.** Some colleagues may want to leverage your experience in work that they are doing and seek your help in making their work product better. Extending an open hand to colleagues by offering to sit down with them and help them better get their point across through their work product is an outstanding means to improving an organization's overall effectiveness. They not only get to benefit from good examples, templates, and tools, but they also get some consulting on their specific work product. Obviously, you need to control how much of this you do and ensure that it doesn't negatively impact your primary job responsibilities. However, I do believe that it is important in any work setting to help others learn and improve. The higher you are in an organization, the more important it is to help those coming up the ranks with you learn and improve. It's a worthwhile investment that pays huge dividends if done well.

If you're a good communicator, share your techniques, tools, and tips with your colleagues.

What if you've got a colleague who needs help but is unwilling to accept it? Well, it's not your responsibility to take on a communications crusade and enforce change on unwilling participants. If the person doesn't want help, don't force it. Do continue, though, to set an example and offer useful templates and tools.

If you're a good communicator, share your techniques, tools, and tips with your colleagues. Not only will you help your colleague, but he or she may make take what you've offered and make it even better. Then your colleague will be sharing his or her knowledge with you. How cool is that?

PART II

THE TRUTH
ABOUT SETTING
DIRECTION

TRUTH 6

DON'T MAKE CREATING A DIRECTION STATEMENT HARDER THAN IT NEEDS TO BE

Vision, mission, goals, values, objectives, and guiding principles. Terms you've heard of but that create confusion within a team when you try to use them to develop something practical. I've been in many strategy meetings where team members have argued over their definitions. "Wait a minute—our mission looks more like a vision!" "Do we need both values and guiding principles?" "I understand what our goals are, but what are our objectives?" These meetings became a classic case of trying to do things right versus trying to do the right thing. At the end, the team felt great because they finally settled on what was a vision versus a mission, and then they promptly forgot about the work that was done in the strategy meeting and went back to doing their job. It's just like spending two days trying to squeeze into size 8 dress shoes when you're a size 10. After you finally squeeze your little tootsies into the size 8s, you take them off and put on your size 10 tennis shoes. Then you hang the size 8s on the wall to show you're in line with company values, but you never try to put them on again because they just hurt too much.

Colleagues, I'd like to debunk a lot of conventional thinking on this topic. Let's cut through the fog and get down to some very practical basics. There are a lot of different opinions on the "right" versus "wrong" way to set and document direction. Frankly, I'm not interested in which way is more right or wrong; I'm much more interested in creating a direction that makes sense to the team and that they can rally behind. Knowing the difference between a mission and vision, between goals and objectives, or between guiding principles and values isn't the important thing. There's no pop quiz here, and I strongly doubt that anyone ever lost his or her job because he or she misquoted a mission as a vision. **Don't make developing a direction statement harder than it needs to be.**

I feel that you need to follow four very simple, basic guidelines to develop a good direction statement:

- You need to know where you want to go.
- You need to know when you want to get there.
- You need to know how you'll get there.
- You need to know what things you'll do to get there.

Think about these four steps in planning your next vacation. You need to know where you want go (Disneyland), when you want to get there (July 4th), how you'll get there (drive), and what you'll do to get there (get gas, stop for meals, check into hotels, break up fighting kids). If all goes as planned, you successfully arrive at Disneyland to see the fireworks, well rested and fed, and the kids are still talking to each other.

Let's take another step and apply this to a mythical pen manufacturer.

Where they want to go:

- *"We want our pens to be in the pockets of every person in the world."*

When they want to get there:

- *"We want our pens to be in the pockets of every person in the world by the end of the decade."*

How they will get there:

- *"We will have the lowest-cost pens on the market."*

What they will do to get there:

- *"We will guarantee that our pens will never leak and will pay the customer's cleaning bill if they do."*
- *"We will reduce our cost per pen by 30% over the next year."*
- *"We will aggressively market our pens to market-leading drug stores, convenience stores, and grocery stores."*

Don't make it harder than it needs to be. Define a direction statement that is meaningful, relevant, easy to communicate, and easy to remember. This is where getting things done and getting your point across happens—not in knowing the difference between a vision and a mission.

TRUTH 7

DON'T BE A CAVE DWELLER

Rio was just promoted to manager of his work team. He was very excited about his promotion. He had wanted this promotion for a long time, and he had worked very hard to demonstrate to his management that he was ready to be a manager. One of Rio's first tasks as a manager was to develop a direction statement for his team. He approached the task with the same zeal that got him promoted and decided to go to his cabin in the woods for some thinking time. He spent three days there thinking about the company, his boss's objectives, his personal aspirations, and where he wanted to take his organization. He came back from his three-day cabin holiday excited and energized about his direction statement and eager to show it to his team. At his next team meeting, he divulged his direction statement to the team. The silence in the room affirmed to Rio that no one objected and that he'd nailed it. Weeks go by, and Rio can't understand why the team isn't showing the same excitement he had about his direction statement. It then occurs to him what the problem is: It was *his* direction statement, not the *team's* direction statement.

Putting together a direction statement isn't just about producing a piece of paper with great words of wisdom. It is as much about how you get to the words of wisdom with your team that makes your direction statement effective. Getting true buy-in means that the team not only needs to agree to the end result, but they need to feel they were

Setting the direction is something that the entire organization should understand, remember, and participate in.

part of the process. When teams understand how you got to the end result and believe they were part of the product, they are much more likely to buy in to the end result and work with you to achieve the results you desire.

To keep from diving into your cave and instead build the buy-in you will need in your direction statement, consider doing the following:

- **Get a 360-degree view of expectations.** Developing your direction statement means talking to your manager, your peers, your customers, your suppliers, and your team about their expectations and perceptions of your organization. Obtaining a 360-degree view of expectations that all stakeholders have ensures that your direction statement is more holistic and better aligns with the direction statements of those you interact with.

■ **Be participative in developing your direction statement.** Setting the direction for an organization is something that the entire organization should understand, remember, and participate in. Include your organization in the direction statement definition process to ensure that you get the buy-in you need.

■ **Give people time to digest.** There's no Minute Rice solution in an effective direction statement. The team will need some time to stare at, think about, and internalize a direction statement. Consider developing the direction statement over a couple of meetings where the team will have some time to sleep on the direction.

■ **Listen and watch for confusion signals.** Questions such as "What does that mean?" or "Why do we want to do that?" are obvious signals that the direction statement isn't sinking in. Also watch the team's faces. Blank stares, furrowed brows, or I-just-ate-a-lemon scrunched faces are signs that the team isn't getting it.

■ **No feedback likely means no buy-in.** I've never seen an active, engaged team just accept and embrace a direction statement without providing some kind of feedback. If your team rubber-stamps a direction statement, they likely won't live by it.

■ **No change is too small if it helps generate buy-in.** I've seen direction-setting meetings spend time on whether there should be a comma, period, or dash separating two thoughts. If something like punctuation helps get the buy-in, let them change the punctuation. Just make sure you watch the other team members to make sure they aren't getting too frustrated with someone who goes on and on about something.

■ **Be cautious about jump-starting the process with your own direction statement.** Depending on the team, this can work well or not so well. If your team is bold, engaging, and not afraid to question, you can probably come in with something and let the team shoot holes in it. If your team isn't as bold or might be afraid to question you, you're better off starting with a blank slate and doing the discovery process together.

Don't go into your cave to develop your direction statement. Talk to your stakeholders, be participative in developing the statement, and watch for resistance or apathy in your team. Getting out of your cave will better ensure that your direction statement has meaning, relevance, and the buy-in you need to get your point across.

TRUTH 8

Lindsay was assigned to head up an organization that appeared to be moving in six different directions at once. The prior manager had been abruptly reassigned to another organization and was already in his new job by the time Lindsay arrived at her new organization. The organization was composed of six teams, each headed by a team leader. Each team leader felt he or she understood the direction in which the overall organization needed to go and was driving his or her respective teams accordingly. On Lindsay's first day on the job, she held a staff meeting with her team leaders. She asked them if there was any kind of direction or mission statement for the overall organization. "Yeah, we did one at our planning off-site at the beginning of the year," one of the team leaders said. "I've got it back in my office; I'll go get it." The team leader brought back the direction statement the team leaders developed at the beginning of the year. Lindsay asked the team if the direction statement reflected what was currently being done. "Well, we had a major reorganization a few months ago, and much of what we were focusing on got prioritized below the work we're doing now." Lindsay asked, "So what are the current priorities that everyone is working on?" Each team leader listed his or her priorities on the whiteboard. Interestingly, there was little correlation between each team's priorities and the direction statement developed at the beginning of the year. The organization's direction statement was useless and was a major factor in the misaligned priorities the team leaders were working toward.

I've both seen this and done it. A team spends hours and hours of effort at the beginning of the fiscal year developing a mission, vision, core values, principles, goals, and objectives. The team agrees on all the strategic components and publishes it as their statement of direction. It then promptly gets put in a drawer, never to see light of day until the team goes through the same exercise next year. In the meantime, the team's execution may follow the direction statement, or it may completely deviate from it. Been there, done that.

Truth is, the direction statement is meant to provide direction and isn't something that should become brittle or stale. If business needs change significantly, which causes the direction statement to need revision, time should be taken to revise the statement. If a direction statement will fail to provide direction, why bother doing one in the first place? Either keep up with it or don't waste the time and money doing one in the first place.

One key problem is as priorities change, many times the direction statement doesn't change with them.

31

Some basic techniques can help you decide if your direction statement needs revising:

- **Compare your direction statement to your manager's direction statement.** A good way to see if you are out of alignment with your organization's direction is to first look at your manager's direction statement (assuming he or she has one). Can you see a direct correlation between the two direction statements? Does your direction statement support your manager's direction statement? If your direction statement is fulfilled, does some part of your manager's direction statement become fulfilled as a result? If you're not aligned with your manager's statement, you need to revise your direction statement.

- **Review your direction statement monthly.** Priorities do change within an organization; one key problem is as priorities change, many times the direction statement doesn't change with them. I've certainly been guilty of creating a direction statement at the beginning of the fiscal year and then never looking at it again. Keep it available, review it monthly, and ensure that it reflects the work being done.

- **Change the direction statement only when the change is material.** True, you want to ensure that your direction statement is current, but you should avoid making minor changes to the direction statement or making changes so frequently that your team and stakeholders become confused by your direction statement du jour. If your organization experiences major directional changes, by all means update the direction statement to reflect the changes.

■ **Compare your direction statement to your performance appraisal objectives.** What objectives are you being measured against? Chances are, you will focus your time and energy on the objectives you are being appraised and compensated against. If your performance appraisal objectives are out of alignment with your direction statement, adjust one or the other.

■ **Look at how you are spending your time.** Look at your calendar. Where are you spending your time? What gets you to work extra early or causes you to stay late at night? If those activities are not supporting your direction statement, either your direction statement is wrong or you are focusing on the wrong things. Either realign where you are spending your time or change the direction statement.

Direction statements are meant to set goals, inspire a team, and align activities. They're not meant to be something that a team should continue to live by when it no longer makes sense to do so. Drive to a direction statement, but don't be afraid to change it once it becomes stale and brittle. An aligned direction statement means that the point you're trying to get across is consistent and focused. Don't get out of alignment.

TRUTH 9

DIRECTION STATEMENTS NEED TO BE LIVED TO BE EFFECTIVE

Think of your current job, or think back to your most recent job or volunteer position. Think about the type of work you perform, who you interact with, what your objectives are. Now think about your organizational direction statement, which may also be called a vision, mission, or goal. Do you know the direction statement? Does one even exist? Do you believe in it? Are your personal objectives aligned with the direction statement?

If you're like most people working in a job or volunteer position, you probably don't know what your direction statement is and aren't aligning your daily work to ensure that the goals in the direction statement are met. Maybe the reason is a poorly communicated or nonexistent direction statement, or maybe it's so high-level and fluffy that you don't know how to relate it to what you do. Or perhaps the direction statement was developed in a cave, and you don't believe in it. Whatever the reason, a direction statement exists for one purpose—to drive an organization's direction. If it's not fulfilling that purpose, it's just wallpaper.

Breathing life into a direction statement doesn't need to be difficult. You've already done the hard work by developing and agreeing on a direction statement. Now you just need some discipline to guide your execution. Consider doing the following:

Keep the direction statement posted where team members can see it.

- **Keep the direction statement prominently displayed.** Too many times a direction statement gets developed and then, after a brief honeymoon period, is filed in a drawer never to see light of day again. Keep it posted where team members can see it. Bring it out during team meetings. Make sure it can be seen and is a constant reminder of what your team is about.

- **Measure your progress against the direction statement.** On a monthly or quarterly basis, provide a status report of results achieved that support your direction statement. Presumably you developed the direction statement to drive your organization toward some results, so why not show the team and other stakeholders how you're doing against what you said you would do?

- **Ensure that your personal objectives align with the direction statement.** You need to set the example and construct your personal objectives (the goals you commit to doing with your manager and on which your compensation and rewards are based) such that they align with and reflect the tone, values, and goals of the direction statement.

- **Ensure that individual team member objectives align with the direction statement.** People will perform based on how they are measured and/or compensated. If you want your team to live the direction statement, make sure their personal objectives align with the direction statement.

- **Orient new team members to the direction statement.** As new team members come on your team, make sure they understand the direction statement and have an idea as to how they will drive their work under it.

- **Adjust the direction statement as the organization changes.** Face it—things change. What your organization had originally set out to accomplish may now be different due to external factors, reorganizations, or shifts in priorities. Don't fall on your sword with your direction statement if it no longer fits into your overall organization. Just make sure you don't get in a mode of making frequent minor changes to a point where the team becomes confused or frustrated with the degree of direction shifting.

You developed a direction statement because you wanted to set a tone of business, inspire the team to perform, and ensure that all were rowing in the same direction. Don't treat the direction statement as a finite activity. Remind the team of your direction, show them what results are being achieved, and don't be afraid to change it when it no longer meets the need.

TRUTH 10

When Others Understand Your Direction, They Can Help You Get There Faster

When I was reassigned to run an organization at a prior company, I decided to go around and interview some of the business partners, customers, and suppliers to understand their needs and perceptions of my new organization. I spent time getting my interviewee list firmed up, my questions documented, and the meetings scheduled. I was expecting to hear things we did well, things we did not do well, and some suggestions for improvement. I arrived at my first meeting with one of my customers and started with my first question. He interrupted and said, "So, what does your organization do?" I was a bit taken aback by the question, since I had assumed it was common knowledge what my organization did. I then spent most of the interview explaining what the group was about and how it impacted my customer's organization. This same thing happened in interview after interview. My key takeaway from the process was that it's great to have a direction statement, but you need to make it available to others and get them to understand it.

You need to let others who interact with your organization know what you do and the value you bring to them.

A direction statement is a formal declaration of who you are, where you want to go, and how you'll get there. If others don't see it, question it, and subscribe to it, you're just like a well-made product that is never advertised. Prospective customers won't know about the product and the benefit it brings to their lives. Publicizing your direction statement is the same thing: You need to let others who interact with your organization know what you do and the value you bring to them. Using your direction statement as a tool to help achieve this is great in helping you craft your message.

Communicating your direction statement among those you interact with doesn't have to be a difficult, time-consuming activity. You can employ some effective techniques to make this happen:

- **Do "who we are" presentations at stakeholder meetings.** Develop a boilerplate "who we are" presentation that explains your organization, what you do, and what you want to achieve. Volunteer to make presentations at stakeholder staff meetings, off-sites, or working sessions. Make sure that the presentation is concise and to the point, and strive to get your key message across in under 15 minutes.

- **Post your direction statement on a website.** If your organization has a website, put your direction statement there. Take opportunities when sending e-mails to include a link to the website either in the body of the e-mail or in your signature. Although some people may not look at your website, it's worth it for those who will.

- **Weave your direction statement into other presentations.** Have a "who we are" slide that you can insert into other presentations. Don't just copy your entire "who we are" presentation into other presentations. Provide a Cliffs Notes-style one-page version for your audience to get enough of a feel for who you are.

- **Embed your direction statement in status reports.** Show results against your direction statement in your status report. Give your audience a flavor of the progress being made by supporting direction statement objectives with key measures and milestones.

- **Put your communication in the context of what it means to your stakeholders.** Apply a little Advertising 101 to your message. Explain to your stakeholders what impact your direction statement has on them and to the overall company or organization at large. The more you position your message as how you help others, the better your stakeholders will understand the value you provide.

Don't keep your direction statement to yourself. Show it around! Let others see what you're about and how you are measuring the success of your organization by reporting results against your direction statement. Make sure you put it in terms that are meaningful to them and demonstrate the value you provide. Others will better understand what you're about and better see what you bring to the organization.

PART III

THE TRUTH ABOUT RUNNING MEETINGS

TRUTH 11

TOO MANY ATTENDEES SPOIL THE MEETING

As a young consultant I was working for a client where we were assigned to reengineer some of its procurement processes. In the middle of our design phase, I set up a meeting with six key managers to review some of the important design changes we were looking to implement. I received positive responses from all the managers, and a couple of them asked if they could bring a lieutenant to the meeting. I didn't see much harm in letting a couple additional people attend. The day of the meeting came and, to my surprise, I had three times the number of attendees I was expecting. There weren't enough chairs, so some people stood. The room was too small for the number of people, and it got quite warm. Despite my having a structured agenda, the meeting constantly got derailed by people asking questions that were inappropriate for the meeting. I emerged from the meeting tired, frustrated, and sweaty (remember, the room was warm!), and I took a big credibility hit with the meeting attendees because I had wasted their time. Had I just controlled the attendee list better...

Meetings can be a very effective means to get your point across, but with a poorly managed and controlled attendee list, even the most compelling points will get lost in red-herring statements like "What is the purpose of this meeting?" and "Can you tell me what this project is about?". Averting the poorly controlled-meeting disaster takes a few simple but effective precautions:

- **Ensure a common knowledge level among attendees.** When you ensure a common knowledge level among attendees, you assess each of your attendees' expected knowledge level of the meeting's purpose and agenda and determine if any attendees are too underinformed to participate. If the meeting is about implementing a policy change, are all the attendees equally informed of current policy? If it is about deciding on choosing a new supplier to provide a critical product component, are all the attendees informed of the reason why the existing supplier is being replaced? If you have any attendees who are underinformed, take some action prior to the meeting to get them informed so that they can participate effectively, or exclude them from the meeting.

- **Keep the meeting to a manageable number of attendees.** Depending on the topic, I generally like to keep my attendee list to fewer than 12 people, with an optimal meeting size of 8 or fewer. If contentious decisions are to be made and ample discussion is likely, it is best to keep your attendee list as small as possible and to only material decision makers. If stakeholders need to be informed of the decisions made, set up a separate meeting after the decision-making meeting to inform them. Avoid inviting them to the decision-making meeting if possible.

- **Prepublish the meeting agenda and purpose.** By prepublishing a meeting agenda and purpose, you do two things. First, you mentally prepare the attendees for the topic and help ensure that they are prepared to discuss the topic at hand. Second, you allow each attendee to determine whether he or she is appropriate for the meeting and let him or her either opt out of the meeting or suggest a lieutenant or peer. Monitor this behavior closely, though, since it may be a symptom of a problem with either the underlying work or with your expected participants.

- **Qualify lieutenant attendees.** Make sure that the lieutenant is not underinformed on the meeting topic. These can be particularly tricky because many times lieutenants attend meetings at the last minute. If you have any lead time, take a few minutes to either call or send the lieutenant information that will help him or her get to the same informed level as other attendees.

- **Take off-topic questions offline.** When you get in the meeting, you owe it to your attendees to stick to the agenda. In doing this, you need to be particularly aware of attendees asking questions that divert the meeting's focus. An innocent question asked in a very nonmalicious manner could cause a meeting to lose its focus and prevent you from accomplishing your meeting objective. If the question can't be

> *You owe it to your meeting attendees to stick to the agenda.*

answered simply and directly, offer to take it offline with the attendee. There are two cautions for doing this. If other meeting attendees have the same question and don't want the topic taken offline, you may need to repurpose the meeting to address the question at hand. The second caution is if the question is coming from a key decision maker who is underinformed compared to other attendees. Do your best to get the underinformed attendee up to speed quickly in the meeting. If you can't salvage the situation, consider stopping the meeting, addressing the underinformed attendee's questions, and rescheduling for a later date. It is better to do this than to waste the time of several people while one person gets educated.

Meetings are difficult enough to control even with an appropriate and informed attendee list. Get your attendee list right, make sure the attendees are equally informed, publish an agenda and purpose, and keep your distractions minimized, and you'll have a more effective meeting where you get done what you set out to do.

TRUTH 12

WATCH THE PONTIFICATOR!

At the offices of one of my clients was a fellow I'll call "Moe." Moe was your typical pontificator. Whenever we saw Moe, he was standing outside someone's cubicle or sitting in someone's office, coffee cup in hand, waxing poetic about the latest dumb decision management made, the idiots who run his division, or last night's baseball game. Moe had an opinion on everything and was very free about letting you know every detail of his opinion. There was no such thing as a 5-minute conversation with Moe. Unless you excused yourself for whatever reason, you were there for at least 15 minutes listening to his philosophy. The problem was that Moe was friends with the person managing our contract, so we had to put up with him.

Moe was particularly problematic during meetings. He diverted agendas, disrupted meeting topics, and wasted tremendous amounts of time. Despite all this, Moe was a long-time company employee and understood his job well. But he was still a big pain in the hindquarters.

It's likely that you've worked with a person like Moe. You do your best to avoid him, but there he is, ready to give you an earful about something. So how do you handle the Moes of the world during meetings? How do you keep things on track? How do you avoid frustrating everyone else in the meeting when the pontificator revs up his engine?

The first thing you can do about the pontificator at your meeting is to take a good hard look at whether he needs to be at the meeting. Will the pontificator contribute content and perspective that will add value to the meeting? If not, avoid having him at the meeting in the first place.

If the pontificator needs to be there, try to talk with him beforehand and solicit his help in keeping the meeting moving forward. Spend a few minutes reviewing the agenda, and get him oriented to the meeting topic. If he has opinions or viewpoints he wants to air, get him to do so with you beforehand, and try to incorporate some of his viewpoints into the topic. If he sees that he has been heard, and if some of his thinking is baked into your agenda, the pontificator is more likely to be a good soldier and not hijack your meeting.

If you've taken this step and the pontificator still feels the need to take control of your meeting, your next mission is to preserve the meeting's purpose, keep things focused on the agenda, and avoid wasting any of the other attendees' time. It is vitally important that you monitor what the pontificator is saying and keep him focused on the agenda item. If he continues to drift off topic onto his own agenda item, ask to have the item taken offline. If it continues, it is completely within bounds to cut the person off and bring things back to your agenda. Whatever you do, **don't lose control of the agenda**. Your credibility is at stake with the other meeting attendees; losing control of the agenda means a loss of credibility, which you'll need to work to regain.

Pontificators don't have to spell doom and gloom for your meetings. If you can ensure that they truly need to be involved in the meeting, get them on your side, and control them when they veer off path, you can still get things done when they are involved.

TRUTH 13

DRIVE A TIGHT AGENDA;
DON'T LET IT DRIVE YOU

A colleague of mine was responsible for running a biweekly two-hour team meeting. He took great care to develop a very full, detailed agenda. As we got into the meeting, we would get through only the first agenda item before the meeting was behind schedule. During the entire time my colleague ran these meetings, we never got more than halfway through the agenda before adjourning. The team got so used to not making it through the agenda that there wasn't even an attempt to stay on schedule. The agenda and its associated times were completely unrealistic and were worthless as a meeting management tool.

An effective agenda goes beyond start time, location, topics, and duration. An effective agenda does the following:

- Supports the meeting's purpose.
- Sets the attendees' expectations of what will be discussed.
- Informs attendees of any preparation that will be required prior to the meeting.

- Gives the meeting leader a road map for driving the agenda.
- Permits adequate time to cover each item.
- Allows the meeting leader to adjust the agenda easily if the meeting gets behind schedule.

As you're crafting your agenda items, make sure that each item supports the meeting purpose.

Having said all this, the meeting owner needs to follow a guiding principle: **The meeting owner drives the agenda, not the other way around.** There are times when you may have a concise meeting purpose and specific agenda items to address, but the actual meeting deviates from the agenda. Be open to the agenda change; just make sure that the meeting purpose is still being met. Doing this requires the meeting owner be very in tune with what is going on in the meeting and bringing it back to what is happening on the agenda. If the meeting is deviating from the agenda, the meeting owner needs to decide if the deviation is appropriate or if it needs to be nipped in the bud. There's no secret sauce for this; it means keeping the meeting's original purpose in mind, observing what is actually happening in the meeting, and continually assessing whether the meeting's purpose is being met.

So what are some good tips for developing an effective agenda? Consider these the next time you have to plan a meeting:

- **Have a tight, focused meeting purpose.** You've called the meeting for a reason; make sure that the purpose is explicit and achievable. A good sanity check on this is that you should be able to complete this sentence: "At the end of this meeting, we should be able to _____."

- **Verify your agenda items support the meeting purpose.** As you're crafting your agenda items, make sure that each item aligns with the meeting purpose. If they don't, either change the agenda items or change the purpose. Don't confuse the attendees by having agenda items that don't support the meeting purpose.

- **Be realistic with allocated agenda item times.** Don't put overly aggressive times on the agenda that you know you won't achieve. Planning 90 minutes' worth of meeting in 60 minutes means you'll get through only two-thirds of the meeting or that the meeting will run over by at least 30 minutes. Don't wish for the best case; put reality down.

- **Distribute the agenda at least one day before the meeting.** Meeting attendees want to know what will be discussed and if preparation is needed beforehand. Give them a day if possible to review the agenda and get mentally prepared for the meeting.

- **Put the most important agenda items at the beginning of the meeting.** Cover your top items first. There are two reasons for this. First, you'll ensure that the most important items get covered. Second, you'll keep attendee attention better by covering the most important items earlier. If they are put later in the agenda, you'll see some chomping at the bit as you go through less-important agenda items first.

■ **Have as your last agenda item an "action items review" section.** I've seen way too many meetings where the end of the meeting comes, and everyone leaves, but there is no agreement on what actions need to be taken. In your action items review, indicate what the action items are, who is responsible for each one, and when the action item needs to be completed.

■ **Have a contingency plan in place for when agenda items run over.** Even in the best-planned meetings, sometimes agenda items take longer than expected. Have a plan for how you will accommodate the change, which could mean shortening or eliminating other agenda items.

Build tight, realistic, achievable agendas. You'll get more done, reduce attendee frustration, and make the best use of everyone's time. Just don't be a slave to the agenda if you see it won't accomplish the meeting's purpose.

TRUTH 14

ONE LESS MEETING GETS YOU
HOME IN TIME FOR DINNER

A client of mine absolutely loved to have meetings. Regardless of the topic, if there was some reason for at least two people to have any kind of interaction, a meeting got called. Not only were there a lot of meetings, but there would almost always be superfluous bodies taking up space in the meeting who had no real reason to be there other than to be "informed." Now, if decisions got made and things got done, I would have had more tolerance for the meeting mania. But more often than not, little got done at these meetings other than to schedule more meetings. It was madness!

As a senior manager, I could have spent every working hour of every day in meetings.

As a senior manager, I could have spent every working hour of every day in meetings. Me meeting with other managers or my staff. Vendors wanting to meet with me. Meeting with customers. Meeting with other organizations. Meetings to decide what meetings to have or not have.

It was meeting after meeting after meeting. I had to actively control my calendar to say no to meetings that didn't make sense and push back on meetings I didn't need to attend or where we could get work done through other means.

As much as I may grouse about meetings, some of them were necessary, beneficial, and effective. Others were a total waste of time and could have been accomplished by other means. The million-Euro question then becomes, "How do you keep the beneficial meetings and eliminate the wastes of time?" In my experience, there are several situations where meetings are generally more appropriate than other means:

- **Getting buy-in or consensus on a strategy, direction, or decision.** Meet if you have something that requires people being 100% bought in to the solution. For people to be truly bought in, they need to have an opportunity to influence direction, express concerns, or provide alternatives.

- **Team building.** If you want your team to work together better, they need meeting time to get to know each other, to understand their relative strengths and weaknesses, and to want to help each other.

- **Celebrating a success or milestone.** Having an e-party just doesn't work. Let your folks get together for a milkshake and celebrate a successful completion of a project, meeting a critical milestone, or a holiday.

- **Delivering bad news where people will likely have questions.** No one likes to find out bad news by reading a memo. If you have bad news that will affect people directly, get them in a room if logistically possible and deliver the message. It gives people an opportunity to interact and is a more humane and sensitive way to deliver bad news.

What are some effective alternatives to people getting together in a room to meet? Try these on for size:

- **E-mail.** Great for disseminating information and for some decision making that may not be contentious or controversial. Just watch for when a topic does turn contentious or controversial; it's best to take the discussion offline and get a meeting together for the relevant parties to discuss.

- **Websites.** Also great for disseminating information or for getting input.

- **Audio/videoconferencing.** Effective when logistics prevent people from physically meeting or when a person only wants to listen in on a meeting.

- **One-on-one discussions.** Effective when a decision or direction can be made by just a couple of people and then others can be informed through e-mail or websites.

We need to interact, we need to exchange information, and we need to work together to get things done. Avoid falling into the meeting trap. Ask yourself if there are other ways to communicate and get your point across.

TRUTH 15

LET DECIDED DECISIONS STAY DECIDED

Jane was a group manager of a team of six buyers for a large department store chain. Her team specialized in buying housewares, including linens, sheets, towels, and small appliances. Her team met every week to discuss advertised specials for upcoming weeks and any supplier issues the team needed to be aware of. One linens supplier, Patty's Linens, had been having some difficulty with product quality, and the department store was experiencing higher-than-normal returns on the product. Two weeks earlier, the supplier submitted a plan for how it would improve the quality of its product. The department store decided to keep the supplier on for three more months to evaluate its plan and give the supplier an opportunity to resolve the quality issues. With this as a backdrop, we eavesdrop on Jane's current team meeting:

Jane: OK, for the next agenda item, Patty's Linens submitted their improvement plan two weeks ago, and they appear to be performing to plan.

Kasie: I thought we decided to terminate Patty's Linens in favor of Briana's Softgoods.

Jane: No, we decided to keep them on for three more months to give them time to rectify their problems.

Jeff: I think we should cut them loose and give Briana's Softgoods a try.

Kelly: I just had lunch with a sales rep from Trevor's Towels. How about we try them instead?

Jane: Guys, we already made this decision and communicated to Patty's Linens that we would keep them on while they worked out their problems.

Bobby: Well, I know that I agreed at the time, but now I'm not so sure.

Jane (muttering under her breath): Only 3,642 days until retirement....

Decision making is one of the most crucial activities that managers perform in their jobs. Their decisions impact company profitability, the lives of their employees, and the viability of the product or service they offer. Making good, thoughtful decisions is a difficult but necessary part of the job. Decision making during meetings is exponentially more complex, because you are building consensus as part of the decision-making process. Those who can facilitate team decision making effectively are diamonds in the rough in any company.

Where team decision making runs amok is when decisions don't stick and they continue to get raised and questioned after a decision has already been made. Now, I'm not advocating a "stick your head in the sand" approach once a decision is made, but you need to give your decision some time to see if it works.

Continual about-faces will cause you to just mark time in your business instead of moving forward. More important, though, is the impact on your credibility. Each time you undecide a previously made decision, you create doubt in the minds of those you are leading, because they will follow you in a zigzag pattern as opposed to a straight line and see you as wasting time. Chronic "indecision making" will ultimately cause the team to not follow you until they are sure you won't change your mind again.

I've used several techniques to help make sure decisions stick:

■ **Keep a decision log.** When developing a decision log, keep track of the following pieces of information: what needs to be decided, when it needs to be decided, what the decision alternatives are, who drives the decision, what the decision is, when it was actually decided, and when the decision will be reviewed to ensure it was the best decision. Now, this may sound like a lot of "administrivia," but recording each decision is important in ensuring that decisions don't get dropped and that the team is reminded of what was actually decided. The little bit of time you spend documenting the decision will pale in comparison to the wasted time and effort of rediscussing decisions already made.

■ **Allow for vetting of alternatives.** The primary purpose of driving decisions in meetings is to make sure that the appropriate stakeholders have a chance to provide their input and perspective on the alternatives before a decision is made. The meeting owner needs to have the patience and discipline to allow for the

Make decisions as a team.

meeting attendees to vet each alternative, hear opposing viewpoints, and come to a consensus. This requires someone who is very in tune with what is happening in the meeting, can keep things moving, and can "close the deal" to get the group to agree on a decision. I've never been able to come up with a magic formula for how long this can take, but someone clearly needs to facilitate the discussion and move the meeting attendees to decision.

■ **Set a "let's evaluate the decision" milestone date.** Once the decision is made, it's a good idea to set a date in the future at which the group will evaluate the decision and assess whether it was the right decision. Doing this is important for two reasons. It provides a checkpoint to ensure that the decision made was a good one, and it also sets an expectation within the group that the decision will be evaluated at a future date and that the can of worms won't be opened again until that point.

Make decisions as a team, log your decisions, vet the alternatives, and evaluate the decision to make sure it was the right one. Do this and you'll better ensure that the best decisions are made once and not replayed like a bad sitcom.

TRUTH 16

ACTION ITEMS GET DONE WHEN ACTION ITEMS ARE MANAGED

It's 9 a.m. and Kay is preparing for her team status meeting that she would hold later in the afternoon. She requested in the last meeting that two competitor briefs be completed for two new products that will be launched. She has been frustrated in the past because action items that she thought would get done didn't always get completed when she expected. Kay was assuming that Dave and Rachel would work on the competitor briefs since they were the respective product managers for the two products. Kay calls Dave to remind him of the commitment. "Oh, sorry, Kay," Dave says sheepishly. "Was I supposed to have that done today? I thought Nell was going to work on it since she showed some interest in doing competitor briefs. I'll get with her and Diane to start working on this today and will have it done in time for next week's meeting. Thanks for the call." Kay gets off the phone, picks up her stress ball, and rips it in half. "Good thing I have a whole box of these things!" she mutters as she throws the mutilated ball into the garbage and pulls a brand-new one from her stress-ball stash.

The stress-ball thing may be a bit of an exaggeration, but the frustration Kay experiences with delinquent action items is very real for people who manage teams. When you are depending on someone to do something and he doesn't follow through, not only is he impacting his job by not meeting a team need, but he is letting you and the rest of the team down by not living up to his commitment.

Why does this happen? One reason is that there is not a clear expectation of *what* the action item is that needs to be completed. In the meeting where the action was assigned, it could be that there was not a solid understanding of what the action item was or it was vaguely stated. Saying something like "We need to research customer behaviors" isn't an action item; it is someone's wish that some general thing needs to happen.

Another reason is that there is not an expectation of *who* needs to complete an action item. Assigning something to "The Team" means that no one will do it, because there is no personal accountability for getting it done. If the action item isn't completed, it's easy to deflect blame, because no one person was held accountable for delivery.

A third reason is that there is no expectation of *when* the action item needs to be completed. Due dates like "as soon as possible" set different expectations in people's minds. I may see "as soon as possible" as meaning "today," whereas you may see it as meaning "after I get through other higher-priority tasks."

A fourth reason is that there is no *follow-up* on the action items. It's easy during a meeting to launch a bunch of action items, but quite frankly, if people know there won't be any follow-up, they are less likely to do the action item. Why waste time and energy doing something that everyone ultimately will forget about anyway?

You can do some very tangible things to increase action item performance:

- **Think what, who, and when.** When you assign an action item, be very clear in documenting *what* needs to be done, *who* needs to do it, and *when* it needs to be completed. With the *what*, be very clear about what the deliverable needs to be and what it needs to look like. If you can't sketch it out on paper, you probably need to rethink the action item. With the *who*, designate one person to be accountable for the action item who will have to answer if it isn't done. With the *when*, make it a hard date and avoid terms like "immediately" and "ASAP."

- **Summarize and send out meeting notes.** While in your meeting, keep an action item log that documents the *what*, *who*, and *when*; summarize the actions at the end of the meeting; and list the action items in the meeting notes in a section called "Action Items." Avoid embedding action items in the meeting notes where they can get overlooked.

  In your meetings, keep an action item log.

- **Gain a reputation as someone who follows up on action items.** If your meeting is a recurring meeting, make your first agenda item a follow-up on the action items from the last meeting, and ask each action item owner to provide a status on his or her action item. If your meeting was a one-time meeting, do follow-ups via e-mail, where all the meeting attendees can see the status of the action items and what was produced.

- **Publicly recognize action item performance.** Giving an occasional "Way to go!" for action items completed well is effective in helping motivate the team to perform. There's an added bonus if you not only recognize the team member but also let the person's boss know (if you're not the boss). If you are the boss, consider including your boss on the recognition. Just make sure you do this for noteworthy achievements only. Praise that is handed out too liberally or recklessly loses its value very quickly.

Gain a reputation as a person who expertly manages action items. Being concise about the action items, who is accountable, and when they need to be done; recognizing noteworthy performance; and doing follow-ups will hold meeting attendees to task and better ensure that meeting actions get done on time.

PART IV

THE TRUTH ABOUT DEVELOPING EFFECTIVE PRESENTATIONS

TRUTH 17

GIVE THEM A REASON TO LISTEN TO YOU

I've been fortunate enough to do a number of presentations at large conferences. Sometimes attendees have to decide what presentations they want to see because multiple sessions sometimes occur simultaneously. If after a few minutes they see value in a session, they stay; if not, they may get up and leave to try out their second-choice presentation. There's certainly no intent to be rude; attendees are just trying to make sure that they are getting the best value they can. For the presenter, though, this is akin to being yanked off the stage with a cane. Every person you see walk out chips away a bit at your confidence and leaves you one step closer to being a quivering mass of jelly right there on the stage. It can be a very uncomfortable, but also very educational, experience. Trust me; I've been educated on this more than once.

A presentation at its core is designed to do one thing: to ensure that by the end of the presentation someone is smarter about something than he or she was at the beginning of the presentation. A presentation satisfies multiple objectives: to inform, to sell, to influence. But all these objectives have at their core to educate the attendees and teach them something new.

Presentation attendees don't just want to know what your presentation is about. They also want to understand why they should spend their valuable time listening to you. You can do only so much about the value assessment. If you are doing a presentation on the chemical alternatives to artificial photosynthesis, you probably won't attract a lot of people who got through high-school science by the skin of their teeth. However, at a school of botany in a major university, you may be the hottest ticket in town. What you *can* do, though, is take a few steps toward getting a high-impact message across to your audience:

- **Get a very clear understanding of your audience's problems.** If a pervasive problem among your attendees is how to manage business risks, don't do a general presentation on business management with risk management as a by-the-way topic. Consider focusing your message specifically on managing business risks or have business risks as a major subtopic.

- **Be provocative.** Do you have an opinion that flies in the face of conventional wisdom? Or maybe a viewpoint that is different from that of your colleagues? Put it out there! Capture your audience's interest by challenging common beliefs or presenting something that is new, innovative, and creative. Your audience wants to be mentally stimulated, so do it.

- **Have a compelling teaser or summary.** Prepare a short summary (no more than a paragraph) of what your presentation is about and what you want your attendees to learn from the presentation. To test how compelling the summary is, ask a friend or colleague to read it and give you his or her knee-jerk reaction. I emphasize knee-jerk because that is exactly what a prospective attendee will do: he or she will read it and quickly decide whether it is valuable for him or her to attend.

- **Tell your audience very specifically what you want them to get out of your presentation.** If you want someone to learn about chemical alternatives to artificial photosynthesis and how these alternatives will benefit the world in the future, tell them as clearly and specifically as you can. If you're doing a sales presentation and you want a company to buy your product, tell them that you want to demonstrate how your product will clearly benefit them. Just put it out there, and don't be vague or covert in your message; if you didn't want something from your audience, you wouldn't be there.

- **Captivate them in the first few minutes of your presentation.** Just because an attendee is in the room doesn't mean that he or she will stay or give you his or her mindshare throughout your presentation. In the first few minutes, make each attendee want to listen to you. I'm not talking about cute stories about your vacation or an "I'm a lighthouse"-type story. I'm talking about a real-life experience or some interesting factoids that will make someone sit up and want to listen to what you have to say.

Make each presentation attendee want to listen to you.

Getting your point across while delivering presentations is so much more than disseminating information. People have to want to hear what you have to say. Knowing your audience's problems, being provocative, having a clear summary, telling them what you want them to learn, and captivating them early in the presentation will ensure that your presentation message is clear and that they'll have a good reason to spend their time listening to you.

TRUTH 18

ENTERTAINING AN AUDIENCE BREEDS EFFECTIVE LEARNING

Lori was really excited about a seminar she had just signed up for. She was in the midst of a career change and thought the seminar on "How to successfully change careers in your forties" was exactly what she needed. She met up with her friend Lisa, and they showed up for the two-hour seminar with notepads in hand, ready to learn some great things. The speaker, Linda-Lou Lawrence, approached the podium, pulled out a stack of note cards, and proceeded to read 80 slides' worth of information directly from the note cards. Her intonation varied between the musical notes "do" and "re" throughout the seminar (at least she wasn't monotone!). She wouldn't take questions until the end of the presentation and rarely looked up to see if her audience was engaged, puzzled, or awake. Despite her content being very thorough, her presentation was abysmal and a huge disappointment for both Lori and Lisa.

Although the names are fictional, almost everyone can think of at least one presentation they attended where the speaker was incredibly dry and dull. Minutes ticked away like hours as the presenter droned on and on about his or her topic.

It really doesn't matter how good the content is; if it's delivered with all the passion and excitement of watching water boil, you won't get your point across. You need to entertain your audience.

You need to entertain your audience.

True, you need to get your point across, but you need to do it in a way that will facilitate and support your goal, not work against it. When I say "entertain," I am not talking about making a fool of yourself, nor am I expecting you to have the charisma of a Johnny Carson or the wit of a Mark Twain. You can use some simple techniques to make your presentations livelier, more effective, and more entertaining:

- **Be passionate about your topic.** How do you expect an audience to be passionate or excited about something if you don't show passion yourself? Let people know that you believe in what you're talking about. To help with this, role-play giving your presentation as if you are giving the final argument in a trial and you have to convince a jury of your presentation's "innocence."

- **Move around some.** Avoid podiums when you can. Even if I am giving a presentation on a stage with a fixed podium, I move out from behind it and walk around. Use gestures to underscore key points. Watch any motivational speaker talk, and he or she is all over the place. Don't be afraid to wander a bit—just don't do it to the point of distraction.

- **Maintain eye contact with the audience.** Pick out a few people in the audience and occasionally make eye contact with them. This helps in a couple of ways. It is a good feedback mechanism to help you read the audience, and it also makes your presentation feel a bit more personal to the attendees (and yourself).

- **Throw in a little humor.** A little genuine, inoffensive, self-deprecating humor is a great way to mix things up. One bit that I use in presentations is a series of pictures where I made a fool of myself while in the audience of a nationally televised morning TV show. This shows not only that you know how to have a good laugh, but also underscores your being genuine and not taking yourself too seriously. Just be cautious not to destroy your credibility with too much humor and not enough content.

- **Vary your voice speed, intonation, and volume.** We're not robots. We can raise, lower, speed up, slow down, and change the pitch of our voices. Want to underscore a key point? Yell a bit! Want to summarize key messages? Slow down and put some punch behind each word.

Entertaining your audience doesn't have to mean that you need to be someone you're not or that you need to perform like Marlon Brando in *A Streetcar Named Desire*. It just means that you need to let your personality and passion shine through. Before you know it, your message will flow like a dolphin through water.

TRUTH 19

PICTURES AND GRAPHICS ARE GREAT, BUT THEY CAN GET REALLY ANNOYING

You've heard the phrase "A picture is worth a thousand words." The original quotation is "One picture is worth ten thousand words." It was penned by Frederick R. Barnard in an ad in the advertising trade journal *Printer's Ink* in 1921. The phrase wasn't Barnard's sole creation; it was based on a Chinese proverb from an unnamed Chinese philosopher.[1] Barnard suggested that because ads with images are more effective than ads without images, readers should place their picture ads on the sides of railroad cars through Street Railways Advertising Company, of which Barnard was the national advertising manager.[2]

The phrase over time has dropped a 0 (going from 10,000 words to 1,000 words), but the essence of the phrase still holds today. Using pictures to get your point across is consistently more effective than asking your audience to read a lot of words on a slide. The mental imagery that is conjured up during the presentation keeps your audience engaged, makes them work less, and creates a more enjoyable and effective presentation.

Pictures and graphics are great in presentations when they do the following:

- Underscore your message by allowing the audience members to write words in their heads that support your message.

- Free the presenter from "reading a script" and let his or her passion and excitement about the message come through.

- Entertain, energize, and engage the audience, particularly when using moving pictures or graphics (also known as animation) in the presentation.

- Complement or underscore the words in the presentation.

Using pictures in your presentation can be great, but they can also be overused or misused. Be cautious about their use when you're doing the following:

- **When presenting precise technical or financial information.** Sometimes this can be adequately presented using graphs or charts, but if the degree of detail creates either a cumbersome or vague picture, stick to presenting data. I had a colleague who loved to use pie charts to show financial information. Sometimes the pie chart would serve the purpose of explaining the data, but other times there were so many pie slices and they were so skinny that the picture became meaningless.

- **Where the picture is redundant with words already on the slide.** For example, if you have "Turn left on Elm Street" on a slide and you have a picture of a car next to it, ditch the picture. The picture needs to embellish your message and allow the audience to think about your point more deeply. If you put a picture on a slide just because you're trying to meet some picture quota, frame it and hang it on your wall instead.

■ **When the picture doesn't support the message you are trying to convey.** It's bad enough when pictures are annoying and superfluous. It's even worse when a picture has a negative effect on your message and confuses the audience.

■ **When the picture is of poor quality.** Your presentation needs to look polished and professional. Using pictures that are blurry, grainy, or jagged is like going into a job interview wearing a beautiful new suit and old tennis shoes. People will remember the shoes as much as they'll remember you.

■ **When the picture is offensive.** This shouldn't need to be said, but it's absolutely happened. Don't let pictures appear that might offend someone in your presentation. If you need help with this, ask a colleague to look at your presentation and assess if you've crossed the line.

■ **When the presentation will be viewed without your verbal presentation or speaker notes.** At times, a picture is great but needs some verbal cues from the speaker to make it understandable. For example, if there is a picture of a gorilla in a presentation about competitors and you are reading the presentation without benefit of a presenter or speaker notes, your audience probably won't get the context; thus, the picture is worth only one word: gorilla.

Pictures are great in a presentation and can significantly increase the effectiveness of your message. Just don't go wild with pictures. Make sure they help tell or support your story and don't detract from or confuse it.

TRUTH 20

RELAX: THE AUDIENCE IS
ROOTING FOR YOU

The Book of Lists reports that when asked what their greatest fear is, 41% of the respondents listed public speaking, ranking it as the number one fear that people have.[3]

You find out that you have to present to a group of people. Maybe you're one of those 41% who would rather die than speak to an audience. For some, the fear is so paralyzing that they simply would rather quit their job than stand in front of a group of people. I had one employee who so hated being in front of a group of people that she wouldn't even go to the front of a room to accept an award, let alone give a presentation to a group of people.

I'm a firm believer that some people will always have an insurmountable fear of presenting. Unless their job requires that they do presentations, let them be. Presenting isn't for everyone, so you shouldn't put people on the spot if they truly hate presenting and it's not a job requirement.

If it is a job requirement, though, those with a fear of speaking either need to get a new job or have to overcome their fear. Sir Laurence Olivier, one of the greatest actors ever to grace the stage, experienced severe performance anxiety throughout his career.[4] He had to learn to recognize it, control it, and deal with it. And deal with it he did, as evidenced by his Oscar-worthy performances in *Hamlet*, *Othello*, and *Wuthering Heights*, among others.

There's an important point to recognize when giving presentations: By and large, your audience is rooting for you. They want to see you do well and want to leave the presentation raving about you. I've rarely seen anyone delight in someone else's presentation failure (public figures, celebrities, and business competitors aside). Several years ago, one of my employees began giving a presentation and immediately froze. For a few seconds, the audience was silent while they processed what was going on. Then a few people from the audience started encouraging him with "You can do this!" Then the entire room broke out in thunderous applause. All because they wanted to let him know they were on his side and they were rooting for him.

Knowing that the audience is on your side, you can do a few things to reduce your anxiety. Recognize that you'll probably always have butterflies in your stomach, but you can keep them from turning into a swarm of hornets:

- ■ **Let your passion flow.** The audience not only wants to hear what you have to say, they also want to see your passion and excitement about your topic.

The audience wants to see your excitement about your topic.

Allowing yourself to get passionate about your presentation will help get your mind off the audience and more on to the topic you're presenting. You have something important to say, so get up there and say it with passion.

■ **Be the most prepared person in the room.** Knowing your content backward and forward can only help your confidence. The more unsure you are about your material, the greater the likelihood of your panicking during your presentation. Strive to be the most knowledgeable person in the room on your topic.

■ **Have a couple of friendly faces in the audience.** If you can, ask a couple of friends or colleagues to be in the audience, and ask them to sit where you can easily spot them in different areas of the room. As you're presenting, alternate looking at them. It will look like you're panning the audience, but what you're doing is focusing on just one face, and then the other, and so on.

■ **Canvass the room and get used to the feel, lighting, podium, and layout.** Before your presentation, go in the room and stand on the stage or wherever you'll be presenting. Get a feel for where you'll stand, how you'll operate any equipment, and where you'll walk. Think about where you want your friendly faces to sit so that you can easily spot them.

■ **Try to chat with some of the audience before presenting.** As people are coming into the room, do some light chatting with audience members. If you find someone who is particularly friendly, use him or her as one of your friendly faces that you focus on during your presentation.

- **Accept that butterflies happen to even the most experienced of presenters.** As with Sir Laurence Olivier, butterflies just happen. Expect that they'll come, and incorporate them into your presentation preparation.

- **Look for any opportunities to speak.** The more you get up in front of a group, the easier it will get, and the better you'll be able to cope with your fears. Embrace the opportunities; don't avoid them.

- **Take a few cleansing breaths.** Just before you take the stage, right when the butterflies are swarming like bees, take a couple of slow and deep breaths. With each exhale, imagine the butterflies being expelled. You probably won't get them all out, but the slow, deep breaths will help calm you down and save you from starting your presentation like a racehorse leaving the gates.

If doing presentations is a requirement of your job, just remember that your audience is rooting for you and that, while you may never completely get over your nervousness, you can employ some techniques to take the edge off and help you get through the presentation more comfortably.

TRUTH 21

DEVELOP CONTENT ONCE; USE IT A THOUSAND TIMES

Fred was a master at delivering presentations on short notice. He could get a call at 3 p.m. with a request to give a presentation the following morning, and he'd follow through with an outstanding performance that would wow his audience. Fred was a great communicator who knew how to get his point across very well. But it wasn't just his verbal skills; his presentation slides were high-impact, relevant, and supportive of his message. When Fred was asked how he was able to do this, he acknowledged having a well-structured repository of presentations that he could use to stitch together a high-impact presentation very quickly. This coupled with passion for his content area made him a highly effective presenter.

Being able to reuse and recycle presentation content into meaningful messages is an outstanding secret weapon of any presenter or public speaker. When done well, and to different audiences, the presenter can save countless hours using content that he or she is already familiar with to tell tailored stories to individual audiences.

How do some people do this so well? Here are several common characteristics:

■ They develop a good understanding of the key messages they need to deliver for each presentation, and they know how to underscore these messages.

■ Their mind-set in constructing a presentation begins with "What can I reuse?" versus "What do I need to create?"

■ They know where to quickly find other presentations they've done.

■ They understand core aspects of their job very well, to the point where they can apply the core aspects to multiple messages.

■ They have passion about their subject matter.

Does this mean that you need to be a master communicator to be able to quickly assemble presentations? Hardly. You just need to be able to put some structure in place to help with stitching together content:

■ **Keep a repository of your presentations.** Keep your presentations in one place where they are easy to peruse and retrieve. Better still, put them in an accessible place where others on your team can use them (so long as the information isn't confidential).

■ **Borrow someone else's presentation.** See a slide or presentation that you found useful or think you could use in some of your work? Ask the person for it! Imitation is the sincerest form of flattery; the person likely will gladly give it to you.

- **Use consistent backgrounds and fonts in your presentations.** Using consistent backgrounds and fonts makes it much easier to copy slides from one presentation to another without having to rework them. Also make sure to view your presentation in black and white if you'll be printing in black and white. What may look great in color might be very difficult to read if printed in black and white.

- **Don't stretch the usage to a point where the message doesn't match the audience.** Reusing presentations is great; just make sure that the messaging in the presentation matches the audience. If you use the same message for a different audience, you just look lazy.

- **Take a minute to at least change the title page.** It's great to reuse information, but if you can't take a few minutes to change information like taking another company's name off the slides, you've just insulted your audience. Make them feel like the presentation was tailor-made for them, even if all you did was change the title slide from another presentation.

You don't have to reinvent the wheel to have an effective, high-impact presentation. Use what you can from other presentations, and assemble your own story tailored to your audience. Just make sure that your message matches your audience's expectations, and you'll get your point across swimmingly.

PART V

THE TRUTH ABOUT WRITING STATUS REPORTS

TRUTH 22

FOCUSED STATUS REPORTS GET READ; RANDOM ONES DON'T

In all my years in business, I have yet to meet anyone who actually enjoys writing status reports. Status reports are often viewed as a largely administrative activity to show people that you are getting stuff done, to communicate potential problems, and (for some) to cover your butt if problems occur. I admit that I too fall into the camp of those who don't enjoy writing status reports. But I've resigned myself to one thing: Life isn't always about what you enjoy doing. Status reports need to be done, so suck it up and do them.

Status reports don't have to be long, verbose documents that provide an audit trail for the work that was completed in the affected period. A status report, at its core, focuses on the following components:[5]

- The status of financial or key organizational indicators
- The status of key milestones for planned work or projects
- The status of major risks with mitigation strategies being deployed
- The status of major issues with the desired resolution

Financial and key organizational indicators outline the major measures an organization uses to measure its effectiveness. Examples of key measures could include items such as time to fulfill an order, average cost per transaction, number of items shipped per day, or revenue per headcount. Typically, key measures are tracked against some target that management establishes. For example, if a business wants to achieve 250 orders processed per day, the target would be 250 orders per day, and the actual would be reported against the target to measure how close the organization is to meeting its goal (or how far it is from the goal).

The status of key milestones outlines major projects or tasks an organization is working on by comparing planned completion dates to actual completion dates. An organization may also want any revisions to a planned date, which is known as a revised completion date. For example, if an organization is undergoing a project to revise its customer service policies with a planned completion date of May 16, and then it revises the completion date to May 31 and actually completes the project on June 2, all three dates would be included on the status report to show when the task was originally scheduled to finish, its revised completion date, and its actual completion date.

The status of major risks outlines the risks an organization faces and what actions can be taken to mitigate the risk. A great example of this was what many organizations experienced with Y2K. The risk was that there would be some kind of business stoppage because computer systems would recognize the year 2000 as year 00 because of older coding techniques. The mitigation strategy for most companies was to comb through their systems and, for every instance of a two-digit year, to change it to four digits. The result of the mitigation strategy was very clear. Y2K was largely a nonevent because of the successful mitigation strategy deployed worldwide (not that Y2K was just a bunch of hype, as many people think).

The status of major issues outlines key business issues that an organization is currently experiencing and the issue's resolution by the appropriate decision maker. For example, suppose a business experiences a sudden upturn in orders, which prevents it from responding to customer service requests in a timely manner. The business owner may have to decide between hiring additional people to handle the increased order volume, authorizing overtime for existing personnel, and accepting a temporary increase in outstanding customer service requests while the business works through the increased order volume. The decision chosen from the alternatives is the resolution that then closes the issue.

If writing status reports is a requirement of your job, suck it up and do it. Focus your status reports on key, relevant, results-driven organizational indicators, milestones, risks, and issues. Don't fall into the trap of throwing everything plus the kitchen sink into your status reports. You'll just turn off your audience.

Focus your status reports on key indicators, milestones, risks, and issues. Don't throw in everything plus the kitchen sink.

TRUTH 23

COMMUNICATE STATUS IN LESS THAN A MINUTE

Almeera was a very thorough, detailed manager. Her written communication was very factual, accurate, and complete. She left no stone unturned in her communication and documented even the smallest event. If you read one of her status reports, you would get a very clear picture of everything that was happening in her organization. The problem was that no one read her status reports because, while they were very detailed and complete, they were just too darn long, and it took too much time to read all the way through them.

> *One of the more common problems with status reports is a focus on activity versus results.*

Almeera's desire to be concise and efficient took second fiddle to her desire to be thorough and complete. Her status reports just weren't effective.

In my experience, one of the more common problems with status reports is a focus on *activity* versus *results*. Some status reports go into great detail about activities that were worked on in prior periods—what activity was done, who did it, and what interesting things resulted. Then they go into activities that will be worked on in the next period. This is great, but your job is to deliver results, not provide an audit trail of all the work you managed.

Throughout my career I've used a simple reporting format that at a glance lets management know where problems exist and what is being done about them. In this status report format, milestones, risks, issues, and costs are shown using a red/yellow/green arrow schema. Green up arrows signify no problems, yellow sideways arrows signify potential problems, and red down arrows signify big problems. The basic premise behind using this type of scheme is that if management sees any red down arrows, they know there are big problems and can immediately focus on those areas. Similarly, if there are yellow sideways arrows, this is a warning that potential problems exist. Green up arrows mean things are OK and there is no need to focus on these items. As a business owner, seeing a status report with green up arrows meant that I could glance at the status report at my convenience if there was something I was particularly interested in learning about. Whenever I saw red or yellow arrows, that was my signal to look at those items immediately and see if the team expected me to help them or to make a decision.

A sample status report using status arrows looks like this:[6]

ORDER MANAGEMENT AND SHIPPING SYSTEM STATUS REPORT AS OF 1/12/2006

OVERALL STATUS

Schedule (Milestones)	Risks	Issues	Costs
↓	→	↓	↑

KEY MILESTONES STATUS

Status	Milestone	Owner	Key Dates		
			Plan	Revised	Actual
↑	Assemble project team	Dawn Jones	11/1		11/25
↑	Complete design specifications	Kent O'Brien	12/15	12/16	
↓	Complete order management development	Michelle Stephens	2/17	2/28	
→	Complete technical testing	Dale Fleming	4/3	4/11	
↑	Complete user acceptance testing	Bonnie Dentz	5/1		
→	Complete training	Bonnie Dentz	5/15	5/25	
→	Implement system	Paul Brennan	5/22	6/1	

PROJECT RISKS

Indicator	Risk	Mitigation	Owner
↑	Developers are unfamiliar with the new technology	Employ consultants through the development phase to supplement team expertise	Dawn Jones
↑	End users are unavailable for the project team per the project schedule	Provide two-week look-aheads on meeting schedules and confirm end-user attendance for each meeting	Bonnie Dentz
→	The new techno-logy cannot handle the expected volumes	Conduct stress testing on the new technology with anticipated volumes to ensure acceptable performance	Kent O'Brien

MANAGEMENT ISSUES REQUIRING ATTENTION

Indicator	Key Issue	Desired Resolution	Owner	Need By	Status
→	Decision required on whether orders can be accepted without an accompanying purchase order	Permit placement of orders without customer entering a purchase order number	Bonnie Dentz	2/1	In progress

93

MANAGEMENT ISSUES REQUIRING ATTENTION (CONTINUED)

Indicator	Key Issue	Desired Resolution	Owner	Need By	Status
↓	End-user manager is being refocused on other activities from her home organization	Reobtain commitment from home organization on assignment; utilize exec sponsor if necessary	Dawn Jones	1/10	In progress

PROJECT COSTS

Indicator	Total Budget	Estimate at Completion	Variance
↑	$500,000	$485,000	$15,000(f)

By using status arrows in an easy-to-read format, you can communicate your status easily and help your readers zero in on where the problems are without making them hunt through lines and lines of text. Your recipients will also be in a better position to help you, because they'll know where your biggest challenges are.

TRUTH 24

KNOW WHO, WHEN, AND HOW

Remember Almeera, our detail-oriented, thorough status report writer from Truth 23? Well, Almeera was not only detail-oriented and thorough, she also ensured that her status reports went to a very wide distribution of people on a weekly basis. To make sure that everyone got her status reports, she would send them by both e-mail and hard copy via interoffice mail. Almeera spent a tremendous amount of time and energy producing and distributing status reports for a lot of people who either didn't care or didn't want to take the time to read a status report that they got in both e-mail and paper form.

Making your status report content concise and relevant is an important first step to developing an effective report. Locking down the recipients, frequency, and distribution method are your next steps to ensure that you're getting your point across to your recipients.

Let's look at recipients first. The first question to ask yourself about your recipient list is "Who cares?" The cold, hard reality is that while you may think your work is vital to your business, some people just don't care because they have more important things to worry about. It could also be that

The first question to ask yourself about your recipient list is "Who cares?"

some people may need to care because, although they aren't affected right now, they may be affected in the future. In determining "who cares," be cautious not to create too thin of a distribution list, where you omit recipients who truly need to know what is happening with your organization. If you're unsure of who should be included, ask a colleague or your manager to review your list and suggest additions or changes.

Next is frequency. Several factors help you determine how frequently to send a status report:

- **Your organizational standards on distributing status reports (if any).** Some companies have guidelines or established procedures for the distribution of status reports. Try to stick with the guidelines unless there's a strong business reason to deviate.

- **If you're doing a project, the length of the project.** If you're managing a two-month project, sending a status report once a month probably isn't frequent enough to inform the recipients. Typically, sending a status report biweekly may be enough unless there are risks or issues that require more frequent distribution.

- **The speed at which information on the status report changes.** If risks, issues, milestones, and key measures change frequently, increase the frequency of your status reports.

■ **Your recipient's need for status.** Ask your recipients how frequently they want to see a status report, and then take the most common response and produce to that frequency.

Now, on to the distribution method. In today's world, electronic is preferred over hard copy distribution. It's more efficient, less wasteful, and easier to do. With electronic, though, you have a choice between "pushing" information to your recipients via e-mail or some other messaging system and having your recipients "pull" information from a source like a website. Either method can be effective, depending on your organization's culture and practices. Just consider that if you publish your status reports to a website, expecting your recipients to "pull" the information, they might need a reminder to go look at the status report. So, if you are "pushing" an e-mail to remind them to "pull" a status report from a website, you might just as well send them the status report by e-mail in the first place.

When sending a status report by e-mail, consider embedding the report in the body of your e-mail versus attaching a status report document, such as a Word or PowerPoint document. By presenting the information to the recipients right in their e-mail, you save them the step of opening an attachment. More importantly, they are more likely to read it because the information is right there for them to see.

Take the time to determine the "who, when, and how" of your status report. By doing so, you better ensure that the point you're trying to get across gets to the right people when they need it, in a method that's convenient for them to read and take action on.

TRUTH 25

NO ONE READS YESTERDAY'S NEWS

Kevin was a new manager. He was learning how to track milestones, monitor risks and issues, and keep costs under control. He was a quick study and was learning the basics well. When it came to status reports, Kevin was thorough, concise, and relevant in what he reported. He spent a tremendous amount of time working on his status reports. He focused so much on producing perfect reports that he sent them a week after the "as-of" date. The content was great, the recipients were appropriate, and the e-mails were well written. But because the content was so out of date, the status reports were beyond action by the recipients and management.

He focused so much on producing perfect status reports that he sent them a week after the "as-of" date.

Imagine opening the newspaper to look at stock quotes, and the quotes you see are from a week ago. Or going to the sports section and seeing sports scores from last month.

Or getting a status report that documents a significant management issue, only to find out that a project will miss its delivery date because the issue wasn't addressed in time. Getting information late is irritating and frustrating and can be costly to an organization. When it comes to status reports, late delivery of information is very avoidable. So if it is so avoidable, why is it a problem? There are several causes:

- **People make writing a status report harder than it needs to be.** As mentioned in Truth 23, a status report isn't about documenting an audit trail of *activity* within an organization; it is about an organization's *results*.

- **Status report writing doesn't pay the bills or bring in revenue.** Given the choice of getting "real" work done or writing a status report, most would choose getting real work done.

- **People generally dislike writing status reports.** Writing reports, particularly when report writing isn't your primary job responsibility, just isn't fun. Generally it gets done only because it absolutely needs to, not because someone wants to do it.

On a project I managed at Microsoft, we refined our status reporting process to where status reports were sent within 30 minutes of our weekly status meeting. Our status reports were relevant, fresh, and timely. There was no magic, just some discipline and cooperation. Here are some techniques you can apply:

- **Adopt a simple, straightforward status report format.** Use a format similar to the one shown in

Truth 23, which focuses on milestones, risks, issues, and financial/business indicators. It's not about how much you write, but how effectively you get your point across in as few words as possible.

- **Do your status report during your status meeting.** Use the time in the status meeting to update milestones, risks, issues, and other indicators. You'll probably discuss these items anyway, so you might as well update your status report while you're discussing status as opposed to putting it off until later.

- **Be ready to send it.** If e-mail is your preferred distribution method, have a distribution list already set up with your recipients included.

- **Block out 30 minutes after a status meeting to finalize the status report.** While things are still fresh in your mind, take 30 minutes to tie up any loose ends, write an executive summary, and proofread it to make sure it looks good. Once it's ready to go, don't wait; send it. The longer you wait to send it, the more likely you'll forget about it and the greater the likelihood you'll send stale information.

You owe it to your recipients, your management, and your team to send timely status reports that don't contain stale or outdated information. Sending status reports that are not only clear and concise but timely will better ensure that your recipients understand the current project status and will help you with issues you may be experiencing.

TRUTH 26

STATUS REPORTS AREN'T CODE FOR
COVER YOUR BUTT

A manager at one of my clients was a master at playing the cover-your-butt game. Whenever there was a problem in his organization, he always seemed to have some reason or excuse for why someone else was responsible for resolution. His status reports reflected his behavior. His colleagues, management, and even his employees would get ambushed in status reports with respect to the resolution of issues. If something went wrong with delivery of a key project, he took comfort in saying, "Well, I told you we weren't going to make our delivery date in my status report." He viewed his status reports as a get-out-of-jail-free card for taking responsibility for problems in his organization. Not cool.

Let me put this as plainly as I can: Status reports are a vehicle for communicating where you are, what can happen in the future, and where you need help with problems. They are not a vehicle that permits you to defer responsibility for managing your organization when things get rough. True, you want to delegate responsibility and accountability and enlist others to help you solve problems. But at the end of the day, you, as the manager, are still accountable for results, and you need to accept ultimate responsibility for performance. In situations where a problem is outside your scope of responsibility, like a policy issue that needs to be decided by your management, they may own the decision, but *you* are responsible for making sure that the decision gets made on a timely basis.

When writing a status report, keep some basic things in mind to help you avoid playing cover-your-butt:

- **Stick to the facts.** Keep your status reports factual and unemotional when dealing with problems or issues. If an unresolved issue means that a key milestone won't be met, say so. Just don't exaggerate and claim that the sky is falling every time something doesn't go your way.

- **Hold others accountable, but don't go to extreme measures to embarrass.** As a manager, it is your responsibility to hold other team members accountable for results. Just be careful not to use a status report to ambush or publicly attack a colleague. If your colleague isn't delivering results, keep to the facts, and don't draw undue attention to his or her nondelivery. Saying something like "John is killing our project" makes the attack personal and will not help teamwork in the future.

Keep your status reports factual and unemotional when dealing with problems or issues. Don't use them to ambush or publicly attack a colleague.

■ **Tell others what you need from them.** Don't just document a problem; be explicit in telling a specific person what you need from him or her to resolve the issue. Also be cautious about using terms like "management" when making a request. You know who you need help from; be specific.

■ **Don't dump problems on others' doorsteps.** When you have a problem you need help with, make sure you're also doing things you need to do to help resolve the problem. Too many times I've seen time wasted on resolving problems because a manager escalated an issue without first doing enough due diligence on the problem. Do your part first, and then escalate or assign it to someone else once you've exhausted your own resources.

■ **It's still your responsibility to drive resolution.** Just because you bring a problem to light doesn't mean you've absolved yourself from future action. You're still ultimately responsible for resolution, so don't wash your hands of a problem just because you shot up a warning flare.

Status reports are great for helping you communicate where your organization is, what the future holds, and where you need help with problems. Use them as a tool to help you get your point across and get things done. Don't use them as a loophole for nonperformance.

PART VI

THE TRUTH
ABOUT
BRAINSTORMING

TRUTH 27

THERE'S A RIGHT TIME AND PLACE FOR BRAINSTORMING

During one of my managerial assignments, I embarked on doing some planning for the next fiscal year. I scheduled a brainstorming session with the entire organization to flesh out ideas on who we were, what objectives we wanted to establish for the next year, and what we would do to meet our objectives. I sent out a meeting notice announcing the brainstorming session, got a nice big room with plenty of whiteboards, and enlisted a facilitator to help us with the brainstorming. One fact I failed to consider was that the session was scheduled during a time that one of my teams was burning the midnight oil on a project. Some of them asked to be excused from the brainstorming session because of the deliverables they were working on. Those who did attend clearly didn't want to be there, because all they could think about was how they would have to stay late to make up for the time lost during my brainstorming session. Also, because they were tired, they (understandably) didn't have the patience and openness that would have contributed positively to the brainstorming session. As a result, my brainstorming session was a failure, because it was the right thing to do at the wrong time.

Brainstorming sessions are a wonderful means of getting some outstanding ideas on the table and generating ingenious resolutions to tough problems. Some of the most innovative changes I have implemented in my career came as a result of someone's (not me) coming up with a great idea in a brainstorming session and others contributing to the idea to really make it hum. When run well, brainstorming sessions can drive solutions that save organizations significant time, money, and effort. To make sure this happens, though, you need to make sure that the setting is right to conduct a brainstorming session.

Want to make sure that your brainstorming meeting gets off to a good start? Implement the following ideas to get things going smoothly:

- **Set aside a separate meeting time for brainstorming.** Be cautious about combining brainstorming sessions with other topics in the same meeting. Brainstorming requires a different mind-set and patience level than, say, issue resolution or project status topics. Let your brainstorming session be its own dedicated session to let your participants stay focused on the brainstorming topic.

- **Set the participants' expectations that you will be conducting a brainstorming session.** The best brainstorming sessions I've seen have all started with expectations being set with the participants prior to the meeting. Being very clear that your meeting will be a brainstorming session and that you want creative, trailblazing ideas about your topic will mentally get your attendees ready and get them thinking about the topic before the meeting. Any pre-thinking that you can achieve with your participants will help ensure that your brain-storming session is lively and innovative.

Don't combine brainstorming sessions with other topics. Let the brainstorming be its own dedicated session.

- **Consider using blind brainstorming tech-niques.** If you're con-cerned that the team won't be open during brainstorming sessions, consider doing something as simple as asking them to write ideas on index cards, putting the cards in a box, and having the facilitator read and record the brainstormed ideas. This can take a bit longer but can generate more creative ideas due to anonymity.

- **Make sure the environment is conducive to brainstorming.** You want freewheeling, push-the-envelope ideas to come out. Make sure that the room is a comfortable temperature, there's plenty of space where people can stretch out, and refreshments are available. Include lots of whiteboards and/or easels to record ideas. Having anything in the environment that distracts people's attention will impact the creativity you're trying to achieve.

- **Don't brainstorm during times of crisis.** Let's say your team has a crucial milestone they're working on until midnight every night. Scheduling a freewheeling brainstorming session at this time just isn't prudent. Many of your participants might not attend because of the looming deadline, and those who do attend will be thinking that they've now got to work until 1 a.m. because of this darn brainstorming meeting. There will probably never be a perfect time to hold a brainstorming session—just watch out for times of crisis.

- **Schedule brainstorming meetings in the morning.** You want your participants fresh, rested, and relaxed for a brainstorming session. If your participants have had a bad or stressful day, they will be less patient and less cooperative with a brainstorming session. Get 'em after they've had a cup of coffee and before they engage in the day's battles.

TRUTH 28

THERE TRULY IS NO SUCH THING AS A STUPID IDEA

Dr. Spence Silver is probably one of the most famous inventors you've never heard of. His invention ultimately became the basis of one of the best-selling and most popular products in history. Yet after creating his invention, it took years of seminars, corporate evangelism, and an innovative colleague by the name of Art Fry to finally find a use for it. The invention? The glue used for Post-it Notes.

In 1969, Dr. Silver created a highly unusual adhesive that wouldn't dissolve and couldn't be melted. Because of its properties, the adhesive did not stick very strongly when coated onto tape backings. Dr. Silver knew he was on to something, but he couldn't find a marketable use for it. Art Fry, a new product development researcher who had attended one of Dr. Silver's seminars, was very intrigued by the adhesive. One day at church, Fry became frustrated with the scrap of paper he was using as a bookmark because it kept falling out of his hymnal. Fry tried some of Dr. Silver's adhesive, and the Post-it Note was born. Today, more than 1,000 Post-it brand products are sold in more than 100 countries.[7] All this because someone stuck with an idea (pun intended) and continued to pursue it until someone else came along and made the idea better.

The story of how 3M Corporation created the Post-it is the stuff legends are made of, but one can only wonder how things were in the 1970s when Dr. Silver was peddling his new adhesive around the hallways of 3M. Even after Art Fry found a use for the adhesive, there was still skepticism at 3M that the product would be successful, and it was almost killed. But tenacity prevailed, and our everyday life is more convenient as a result.

Brainstorming is a great method of fostering innovation and creativity, but sometimes reality creeps in.

Brainstorming is a great method of fostering innovation and creativity, but sometimes reality creeps in too quickly and sifts out ideas that might be viewed as impractical, impossible to implement, or just plain silly. Applying reality to brainstorming is like asking a chef to create a wonderful dessert but limiting the ingredients she can use. She can still create something, but nothing as spectacular as she could otherwise. Reality leads to constrained thinking, which leads to stifled innovation. Start applying reality too soon, and your brainstorming session will become just a rehashing of old ideas.

You can keep great ideas flowing and potentially find the next Post-it Note by employing some of the following ideas:

- **Don't assess ideas during brainstorming; just get them down.** Don't generate and assess ideas at the same time. Let the idea-generation engine run, and let participants get their ideas out. Just keep writing and encouraging out-of-the-box ideas.

- **Put ideas that don't resonate with the participants in a "parking lot."** At some point you'll need to do something with the ideas you've generated. Some may resonate with participants; others may not. For those that don't resonate, put them in a "parking lot"—a whiteboard or easel containing ideas and thoughts that were generated from the brainstorming activity but that don't have a clear application yet. Don't be too quick to throw them out or hide them from the participants, because they may have a use later.

- **Keep looking at your parking lot ideas to see if some splinter idea comes from them.** Encourage participants to occasionally look to the parking lot to see if an idea spawns from something that came from your brainstorming. Permit participants to express their thoughts and think creatively about the parking lot ideas. Maybe nothing will come of them, but then again...

- **Don't chastise people who think out of the box.** Brainstorming sessions are wonderful playgrounds for out-of-the-box thinkers. Let them climb on the monkey bars and swing on the swings by encouraging them to get crazy with their ideas. Chastising an out-of-the-box participant because of his or her ideas is sure to put a damper on innovation and limit the effectiveness of your brainstorming session.

■ **Don't be too quick to dismiss an idea that doesn't resonate with the participants.** If, after doing initial brainstorming, the participants don't seem to latch on to an idea, don't jump the gun and dismiss the idea. Put it in a parking lot and let it percolate for a while. Something else may come of the idea, or the other participants may begin to see some merit in it.

Brainstorming sessions are tremendous ways to generate innovative, creative, groundbreaking ideas that can reinvent a business, volunteer organization, or any other setting where a group of people need to get something done. Promote the innovation and creativity by keeping all ideas in the forefront or in a parking lot and letting your out-of-the-box thinkers have a field day. You never know what golden nuggets will come out of the brainstorming session.

TRUTH 29

BRAINSTORMING ISN'T CODE FOR A WASTE OF TIME

I attended quarterly meetings in one of the organizations for which I do volunteer work. The meetings would start with a very nice dinner, and then there would be some general announcements, and then the participants would break into individual task groups. My task group was headed by a very nice, thoughtful person who truly wanted to do the right thing and make his task group better and more effective. At each task group meeting, we would spend time brainstorming new things we could do as a task group to better interest and reach our customers. This meeting became my own personal version of the movie *Groundhog Day*, in which Bill Murray awakens each morning to find that he is living the same day repeatedly. We would brainstorm some ideas, and the task group leader would write them down, praise us for all the great ideas, and dismiss us. At the next meeting we'd do the same thing all over again. I ultimately stopped going to the meetings because they became a colossal waste of time.

You probably have a story similar to this or may have your own horror story of a brainstorming session gone bad. The frustration gets amplified when you need to work overtime to get other work done to make up for the time you lost attending a yucky brainstorming session. It takes only a couple of bad brainstorming sessions for participants to see a pattern and for you to get a reputation as a time waster when it comes to brainstorming.

Take heart! Brainstorming sessions don't need to be high-risk ventures that tarnish your reputation. You can put some strategies in place to help make sure your brainstorming sessions provide value and do what they are intended to do, which is generate great ideas:

- **Outline an agenda for the brainstorming session.** Put together a simple agenda that tells participants how much time you will spend generating ideas, voting on ideas for further pursuit, and crafting the next steps. True, you're putting some structure to an unstructured event, but your participants want to see that structure to give them some assurance that their time isn't being wasted.

- **Set a defined time when you'll brainstorm.** Keep your brainstorming sessions quick and intense. The best brainstorming sessions I've done have lasted less than an hour, including idea generation, voting, and next-step crafting. If participants know you are trying to run a sprint, they will prepare for a sprint and not a marathon.

- **Save brainstorming for when you need to generate ideas.** Don't use brainstorming as a team activity or a reason to get people together. Brainstorming is a specific activity with a specific purpose—to allow participants to get really creative in generating ideas that solve some problem.

■ **Outline your plan for what you'll do with brainstormed information.** At the end of your brainstorming session, define specific action items that outline how the brainstormed information will be used and what will be done

> *Don't use brainstorming as a team activity or a reason to get people together.*

with the ideas generated. Include the participants in the action items to keep them from feeling as if the great ideas are just going into a black hole, never to see light of day.

■ **Let people be either participants or facilitators; don't ask them to do both.** Participants are expected to contribute ideas and provide perspective; facilitators are expected to record ideas, cull the ideas that require future action, and set the action plan. Asking someone to do both constrains the facilitator from contributing his or her ideas and can introduce bias into the brainstorming process. Give your participants a break and let them be participants.

■ **Construct tangible, defined next steps you'll take with the brainstormed information.** Don't frustrate your participants by dragging them through a brainstorming session only to have no tangible actions come out of it. Let the participants know what will happen next and how the brainstormed information will be used.

- **Set a time to follow up with the participants on how the brainstormed information is being used.** Define *what* is important when outlining actions. Defining the *when* sets an expectation of when the actions will occur and gives the participants greater confidence that something tangible will happen because of the brainstorming session. Do follow-ups with the group so that they can see progress being made.

Let the participants know how and when the brainstormed information will be used.

Instill structure, focus, and follow-up in your brainstorming sessions. Your participants will feel as if their time wasn't wasted and that tangible actions will be pursued as a result of the session. Participants will remember if you wasted their time and may not attend your next brainstorming session to avoid another time-wasting activity.

TRUTH 30

BIASED FACILITATORS TORPEDO
BRAINSTORMING SESSIONS

I was a manager of a group of fairly experienced managers who were pretty set in their ways and who didn't venture to the deep end of the creative-thinking pool. They were very good at what they did and were fairly resistant to change, particularly self-inflicted change. As I was thinking through some structural changes for the group, I decided I would participate and set up a brainstorming session to generate ideas on how we could better structure ourselves to meet our customer needs in the future. I decided I would facilitate this brainstorming session myself to ensure that I got what I wanted out of it. I did all the right things in setting up the session: I scheduled it well in advance, I ensured that no one was involved in a crisis deliverable, I found a great room, I stocked it with plenty of markers and easels, and I had refreshments at the ready.

When the meeting started, I kicked off the brainstorming session. It was very clear to the group I was looking for a specific outcome—to make changes. Because my focus was on change, I inadvertently biased the participants. They were more focused on trying to anticipate the types of changes I wanted than on thinking purely about the business and what changes would be best for our customers. The end result of our session was a lot of ideas the participants thought I wanted to hear, as opposed to breakthrough ideas they could have expressed on their own. By facilitating the brainstorming session and injecting my own biased thinking, I unduly influenced the group's participation and ended up with a bunch of marginal ideas. Good intention, poor outcome.

> *By facilitating the brainstorming session and injecting my own biased thinking, I unduly influenced the group.*

Getting your brainstorming meeting logistics set up and ready to go is a good idea to ensure that your session gets off to a good start. Employing a strong, unbiased, experienced facilitator to drive your session is important to ensure that you have a strong finish. The most effective facilitators are great at promoting an open, inclusive environment, keeping their own bias in check, and getting participants to stretch their thinking by asking questions that challenge the status quo. The right facilitator can poke and prod and bring out great ideas that participants might not have come up with on their own.

Ensure that you have an effective, facilitator-driven meeting by doing the following:

■ **Ask someone to facilitate who has no stake in the outcome.** You want your brainstorming session to be inclusive, open, and objective. By using a facilitator with no hidden agenda or stake in the outcome, you ensure that bias doesn't enter your session and that items don't get excluded or omitted through the facilitator's own slant on things.

■ **Use an experienced facilitator.** Some people are good at this, and some aren't. The important things are that the facilitator knows how to ensure inclusion and that he keeps things moving forward. You don't want someone who keeps generating ideas without going through the step of narrowing them down.

■ **Encourage the facilitator to push the envelope.** A good facilitator challenges the participants to broaden their thinking and question the status quo. Asking open-ended questions that start with "What if...?" or "Why not...?" helps the participants question how things are done today. This prodding just might generate a new stream of thinking that gives you a breakthrough idea.

■ **Don't "stealth-facilitate" the session.** Regardless of who is facilitating, the manager or most senior person in the room can still be the man behind the curtain, pulling ropes and pushing levers to make the room come to his or her point of view. The senior person needs to avoid verbal and nonverbal cues that cause other participants to alter their comments.

You want to take as much bias out of your brainstorming session as you can to keep from getting bogged down on a specific point. You also don't want to start applying reality too early and sift out potentially great ideas. Use an experienced facilitator who has no stake in the outcome, and you will better position your brainstorming session to generate awesome ideas and breakthrough thoughts.

PART VII

THE TRUTH ABOUT PROBLEM SOLVING

TRUTH 31

EVERY SOLUTION NEEDS A PROBLEM

When it came to raising problems, Joe was the king of the castle. Regardless of size or magnitude, if something was wrong, Joe would find it and let his colleagues know. "We need to fix how we schedule our production workers!" "We need to stop cutting corners and buy better computers for all of us!" "There are never any pens in the supply room!" "Management doesn't know what's going on!" The problems would go on and on. It also seemed that the latest problem Joe found was now the most important problem to solve, regardless of its impact or the benefit that would be achieved. Despite Joe's seemingly good intentions to highlight issues that needed resolution, the problems were so poorly articulated and prioritized that they were not actionable.

Getting a clear understanding of the problem you're trying to solve is the most important first step you can take to drive a valuable solution. Too often, our problem definition stems from frustration with the current state of affairs and, taken in its raw form, is an emotional statement rather than a factual one. For example, "Management doesn't know what's going on!" is an emotional response to someone's frustration with the status quo. You'd have better luck playing the lottery than trying to come up with a solution to this problem as currently stated.

Coming up with a well-defined problem statement means putting the statement through a few paces:

- ■ **Dig deep to find root causes of the problem.** Make sure you're solving a root-cause problem and not purely a symptom or a consequence of the root cause. Let's look at an example. Say your problem is "I can't seem to get my work done on time, and my boss is getting ticked." Let's ask a few "why" questions to dig into the problem:

> *Too often, a problem definition is an emotional statement rather than a factual one.*

Why are your assignments late?

Because I don't find out about them until last minute, and I have to rush to get them done.

Why don't you find out about your assignments until the last minute?

I find out about them from e-mail only a couple days before they're due.

Why is e-mail the way you find out about your assignments?

Because that is the only way I interact with my boss.

Why is e-mail the only interaction with your boss?

Because he keeps canceling our weekly one-on-one meetings.

Why does he keep canceling your meetings?

Because I never give him an agenda of things to discuss beforehand, so he assumes we have nothing to discuss.

Ahhhhhhhhhhhh *haaaaaaaaaaaaaa*! So the original problem statement of "I can't seem to get my work done on time, and my boss is getting ticked" is only a consequence of the true problem of "My weekly one-on-one meetings keep getting canceled because I don't submit an agenda beforehand." A little bit of digging will unearth golden nuggets—just pull out a shovel.

■ **Write down the problem in concise, actionable language.** If you can't put pencil to paper and clearly articulate the problem you're trying to solve, how can you expect to devise a solution? Take a few moments to write down the problem in clear, concise, actionable terms.

■ **Get some consensus on your articulation of the problem.** Once you've written down your problem, ask a couple of colleagues familiar with your situation to cross-check you. Ask them to do some "why" questions on your problem to help you dig down and get to some root causes.

■ **Gain agreement that the problem is big enough to do something about.** You may do a good job of articulating your problem, breaking it down to root causes, and getting some consensus on the problem's authenticity. Now you must decide whether it's a big enough problem to take action and resolve it. For example, our clothes dryer sometimes stops in mid-cycle for some inexplicable reason. Because it is so infrequent, and all you have to do is start the dryer again, we elect to just live with it. It's a problem, but it's not a big enough problem for us to do something about.

Good problem solving starts with a crisp and actionable definition of the problem you're trying to solve. Gaining a strong understanding of a problem's root cause and how important it is to solve the problem will help set you on the road to being an effective problem solver.

TRUTH 32

CHOICES AND CONSEQUENCES
MAKE THE SOLUTION

One of my client companies conducted a software selection project to help it choose a replacement for its old purchasing system. The client project manager was a long-time employee of the company and had worked on its old purchasing system for years. He had a lot of time invested in the old purchasing system and didn't believe the company needed a new one. We went through an evaluation process where we looked at business requirements and system features to assess how each system fit the requirements. To ensure we were making a good business recommendation, we also assessed the old purchasing system against the requirements to see how well the old system fit relative to the newer systems. The client project manager intentionally "stacked the deck" on the requirements list to include requirements he knew only the old purchasing system would be able to meet. To no one's surprise, his recommendation to his management was to continue using the old purchasing system because it best met the requirements of the business and was the most cost-effective solution. Unfortunately for him, his bias came through loud and clear, and he was sent back to the drawing board to redo the evaluation with more objective requirements and evaluation criteria, which subsequently yielded a different answer.

You must clearly define the problem being solved and thoroughly understand the choices and resultant consequences.

Arriving at good, reasonable business decisions requires not only a clear definition of the problem being solved, but also a thorough understanding of alternatives, or *choices*, that can be chosen and the resultant *consequences* an organization faces for each choice. For example, let's say it's quitting time at work and you're trying to decide on the best route to drive home. The problem you are trying to solve is that you want to get home in the shortest amount of time. If you take the freeway, your drive will be 12 miles, and the average drive time will be 20 minutes. If you take city streets, your drive will be 10 miles, and the average drive time will be 30 minutes. Your choices and consequences are as follows:

Choice	Consequences
Take the freeway home.	The drive is 12 miles. The average time is 20 minutes.
Take city streets home.	The drive is 10 miles. The average time is 30 minutes.

In looking at your problem statement, you want to get home in the shortest amount of time possible, so from a priority standpoint you are willing to drive more miles if it means getting home earlier. Given this criteria and the outlined consequences, you decide to take the freeway home because, although it is a bit longer, on average you'll get home quicker than by taking city streets.

To help you outline the choices and consequences for your problem statement, use the following guidelines:

■ **Decide on your evaluation criteria.** Depending on the factors surrounding your problem, you may have different evaluation criteria that drive each proposed solution. For example, in the case of one project I worked on, speed and adherence to requirements were more important than cost. Thus, as we evaluated each alternative, we kept an eye on costs but were willing to pay more for a solution that had a faster delivery and better met requirements.

■ **Articulate the factual consequence of choosing each alternative.** My preference is to list factual consequences for each alternative as opposed to having separate columns for pros and cons for each alternative. I've found that it is too easy to inject bias into your analysis by having a longer list of either pros or cons. You could have five pros and only one con listed, and your first impression might be that the pros outweigh the cons by 5-to-1 due to assuming that all pros and cons have equal value. However, if the one con is "the solution won't be available for three years" and you need it next year, that one con is probably a deal-breaker.

- **Consider using a numbering scheme or arrows to rank each criterion against each alternative.** For each criterion you've identified, apply some kind of visual ranking to show most- to least-favorable alternatives. I'm not suggesting getting fancy with math and coming up with weighted average scores or some other quantitative evaluation method unless that is part of your organization culture. Whatever you do, present it in simple terms that facilitate good decision making.

- **Keep it objective and factual.** Watch your own bias. You may have a favorite solution that you'd like to see implemented; just make sure your analysis of alternatives doesn't show the bias. Stick to the facts.

Define thoughtful, practical alternatives to your problem statement, and clearly outline the consequences of each alternative. Make sure the evaluation criteria you use are accurate and realistic, and keep things factual. You'll get your decision alternative points across and better ensure you're making a good decision.

Truth 33

Dig Hard for That Third Alternative

It was 10 p.m. and Matt and Chris were sitting at the conference room table exhausted and bleary-eyed. They were preparing for a presentation at 8 a.m. the next morning with the vice president of their division and were quickly approaching a panic state. They were staring at a Choices and Consequences slide they had created to evaluate alternatives for reducing costs in their organization. "These alternatives stink!" Matt grumbled. "We either have to forgo hiring five people we had planned to hire or spend a lot less on systems. Either way, we'll never meet our service agreement with our customers, because we'll be forced to do more with less. I feel like we're just choosing the least-worst alternative at this point." "I feel your pain, man!" Chris echoed. "Either way, we're screwed." They believed this was the best they could do and decided to go into the meeting, present the information, and let the vice president make the decision for them.

The next morning Matt and Chris went into the meeting and laid out their two choices and the consequences for each. The vice president asked whether they had considered renegotiating their service agreement with their customer so that they could reduce the number of people required to meet an agreed-upon level of service. By taking this approach, they could potentially forgo hiring the five additional people for the department and still implement some of their planned systems changes while still meeting their customer's expectations. Matt and Chris looked at each other sheepishly and admitted that they never considered that alternative. "Well," snapped the vice president, "how about you do some more homework to see if this alternative would work?" Matt and Chris hightailed it out of the vice president's office. They ultimately renegotiated their service agreement with their customer, which allowed them to cut their costs while keeping their customer happy. Ah, the magic of the third alternative!

Good, foundational mainstream thinkers can identify basic alternatives, outline the consequences of each path, and present information so that management can make an informed decision. However, it's the great, innovative, out-of-the-box thinkers who can see past the obvious, basic alternatives and come up with alternatives that may be a bit out of the mainstream but are a better solution than the basic alternatives. These are the types of solutions that spur excitement in an organization, because they're unique, innovative, and typically fun. Now, I'm not saying that every solution has to be a magical third alternative-type solution. If a basic solution solves the problem acceptably, by all means go forth and conquer. But if you find yourself not liking any of your proposed solutions and are faced with choosing a least-worst solution, it may be worthwhile to dig deeper to see if a third alternative exists.

One question that comes up in this arena relates to creativity. Not everyone is creative or innovative. Their strengths may be in other areas. Does this mean that you're forever trapped in basic-alternative land? Nyet! This is where the power of leveraging colleagues or others you know are creative is crucial. If you're not a creative thinker, find one you can tap to help think through alternatives and dig up some creative ideas.

Innovative thinkers can see past the obvious alternatives and come up with choices that may be a bit out of the mainstream.

To help find the third alternative, consider some of these ideas:

- **Do a mini-brainstorming session to identify potential alternatives.** If you need to generate some ideas on solutions, get a few colleagues in a room and do a mini-brainstorming session. Be sure to choose people you know are familiar with the problem and have a reputation for being creative and innovative.

- **Dig for hybrid alternatives that take the best characteristics of the others, and create a new alternative.** Take a good hard look at the alternatives you already have outlined, and think about how they could be combined or redesigned to come up with a new choice that contains the best characteristics of each alternative.

■ **Use a more experienced person or mentor as a coach.** Some of my most creative solutions to problems came from reviewing alternatives with one of my mentors, who helped me come up with a more creative third alternative. Don't worry about appearing weak or inferior when asking a more senior person for advice. One of that person's responsibilities in the organization is to help those coming up in the ranks behind them be more effective employees.

■ **Ask around.** Shop your alternatives around to a few colleagues, and ask them to help you think through other potential alternatives. Just as with mini-brainstorming, pick a couple of colleagues who are both familiar with the problem and creative.

When fleshing out alternatives, you don't always need to choose column A or column B. Spend a bit of time looking in column C. Any digging you do might just be well worth the time if it yields a more creative, innovative, and effective solution.

TRUTH 34

A SOLUTION IS ONLY AS GOOD AS ITS IMPLEMENTATION

Brody was feeling very good about the solution his organization had agreed to implement. He had developed an outstanding "choices and consequences" analysis, had identified relevant evaluation criteria, and had driven the decision in a very participative manner. In the meeting where the organization decided on the solution, Brody had outlined some actions needed for the team to implement the solution. He rattled off some general actions and said, "We need to get these done as soon as possible." Feeling great about his success, Brody went home and took his wife out for a fancy dinner and dancing.

After two weeks, Brody was getting concerned. "I hope the team is working on implementing the solution," he thinks. He starts calling people he thought were working on his action items. "Oh, was I supposed to own that?" one says. "I thought Dana was doing that," he hears from another. He realizes that, although everyone was clear on the solution to be implemented, they weren't clear on who was supposed to do what. He didn't get his point across on implementing the solution.

Making an informed, thoughtful, difficult decision can generate feelings of relief and excitement that you've navigated the rough waters of decision making. This is tough stuff, and you should take a minute to grab a milkshake and enjoy the moment. You need to start working on the next phase, though, which is solution implementation.

> *In implementing a solution, be clear about what needs to be done, who needs to do it, and when it needs to be done.*

In implementing the solution, you need to be very clear about what needs to be done, who needs to do it, and when it needs to be done. It's your responsibility to ensure that people know what is expected of them and to follow up to ensure that action items get done.

When implementing your decided-upon solution, keep the following in focus:

- **Delineate specific actions.** To implement the chosen solution, you probably need to take action. Once the decision is made, delineate the specific actions to take. Ensure that the actions are clear and that each action produces a tangible deliverable.

- **Assign ownership to actions.** You've defined the *what*; now define the *who*. Assigning tasks to an organization or "the team" means that the action probably won't get done. Assign someone to each action if you want it to get done.

- **Assign due dates to actions.** Set the expectation that actions need to be completed by a specific date. Putting dates such as "ASAP" or "future" does not set a clear expectation of when the work needs to be done. Pull out your calendar and pick a date.

- **Set a follow-up date to review actions.** Agree to some date in the future where you will get together with action owners and other key stakeholders to review progress on action items. If action owners know they will be held accountable in a public setting, they are more likely to get the action items done.

- **Document it.** Send meeting minutes documenting the proposed solution, action items, assignments, and due dates to meeting attendees. Remember to include anyone who was "volunteered" to own an action item but who wasn't at the meeting.

- **Set a date to evaluate the solution.** Just because you made a decision doesn't mean it was right. It's possible the solution path you are pursuing is the wrong path. Set a date in the future when you will evaluate your decision and either proceed with the solution or do an about-face and choose another path.

Making decisions can be hard business, but getting your solution implemented can be even more difficult, particularly if you rely on others to make it happen. Be clear about what the actions are, who needs to do them, and when they need to be done. Diligence in your follow-up on the solution implementation will ensure that you're getting your point across in solving the problem.

TRUTH 35

BAD DECISIONS THAT DON'T GET FIXED GROW INTO DISASTERS

As a young manager, I was put in charge of managing the development of some major enhancements to a purchasing system. I did all the things a good project manager does in planning the project, securing resources, and publishing a schedule. The project immediately got behind schedule, and we were faced with the decision of cutting some of the enhancements or staying the course and trying to make up lost time. I decided to stay the course and work the team harder to make up lost time. The project continued to fall behind schedule, and I continued to push the team to get back on schedule. The team, my colleagues, and my management were all telling me that what I was trying to do simply couldn't be done in the time allotted, but in my arrogance I pressed forward. I ultimately was removed from the project, and a new project manager was appointed. He promptly revised the schedule and cut some of the enhancements to bring the project back to reality. My bad decisions and unwillingness to listen ultimately cost me my position on the project. This was a great lesson learned.

Making decisions is something we all do every day. Deciding what to eat for lunch, what to watch on TV, or whether to exercise or sit on the couch with a bag of potato chips are routine, common decisions that are made lightly and with little regard for the consequences.

> *My bad decisions and unwillingness to listen ultimately cost me my position on the project.*

Some decisions, though, have greater consequences that require evaluating the decision for a period of time. Let's take the decision to sit on the couch and eat potato chips versus exercising. Over time, you will likely gain weight, increase your cholesterol level, and put your health at risk. Left unchecked, this decision could ultimately affect your life. By putting some criteria in place, like stepping on a scale once a week and noticing the notch where your belt is buckled, you can evaluate your decision to be a couch potato and start hitting the gym when you notice additional pounds around your midsection.

This is a simplistic example (and one that most all of us can relate to!), but the concepts here are the same whether you're watching your waistline or making decisions that affect your organization. The decisions you make need some feedback mechanism to ensure you've made a good decision and to give you the opportunity to change course when things go wrong. When you put a feedback mechanism in place, you mitigate the risk of your decision's negatively impacting your organization, and you give yourself time to recover if the decision was poor.

There is a deeper issue to consider in this area as well—credibility.

When you admit you made a mistake and you put measures in place to fix it, your credibility with colleagues, employees, and management skyrockets. It shows that you are willing to put doing the right thing for your organization over and above doing the right thing for yourself. Putting the organization or others first tells those around you that you aren't just in it for yourself. Believe me, people notice who puts the needs of the organization above his or her own personal needs. Such people carry very high degrees of credibility.

When you admit you made a mistake and put measures in place to fix it, your credibility skyrockets.

What can you do to help your decision feedback mechanism run smoothly? Give the following ideas a look:

- **Put a follow-up plan in place to evaluate the decision.** Determine a good time frame to come back to evaluate the decision. The time frame is up to you. If you're unsure of an appropriate time frame, ask your action item owners and stakeholders for their opinions.

- **Define specific criteria that help you measure the decision's effectiveness.** Define quantitative measures that help you determine whether your decision is delivering the results you expected. Squishy statements like "things are going well" are nice feel-good statements but don't do anything to help stakeholders understand the decision's effectiveness.

- **Keep it factual, not emotional.** Be diligent about making factual statements about your view of the decision's effectiveness. Being factual doesn't mean you can't have passion. By all means, be passionate about what you're doing, and let people know you're excited about the benefits the decision will bring. Just make sure your passion is backed up by facts.

- **Don't be the last to know the decision was wrong.** Passion run amok can lead to your getting emotionally tied to the decision and doing everything you can to save a potentially bad decision. If others are telling you that the solution isn't working and you need to revisit the decision, listen to them. Be among the first to know you need to do an about-face, not the last one to be convinced.

- **When you have to reverse the decision, do it swiftly and deliberately.** Changing direction isn't fun, but when it needs to happen, execute aggressively. Accept the situation as a good learning experience and pursue plan B. Don't brood or drag your feet.

Admitting that you drove a wrong decision isn't fun, but stuff like this happens, and you need to suck it up and deal with it. Define when and how your decision's effectiveness will be evaluated using factual information. If you need to about-face, do it deliberately and swiftly to get on the right path. Making bad decisions isn't nearly as bad as sticking with bad decisions. Turn it around before it bites you.

PART VIII

THE TRUTH ABOUT INTERVIEWING

TRUTH 36

YOU CAN'T OVER-PREPARE FOR AN INTERVIEW

A colleague and I were interviewing some upcoming college graduates on a university campus. Most of them were very prepared, looked presentable, asked great questions, and seemingly had done their research. There was one, though, who stood out from the rest, and not in a good way.

Out of the gate I knew this would be an interesting interview. The interviewee showed up 10 minutes late for his interview. He looked as if he had just crawled out of bed. He had on an old sweatshirt, jeans, and sandals, and he hadn't bothered to brush his hair. He hadn't researched my company, didn't understand what products we developed beyond our flagship product, and didn't know what types of jobs we were looking to fill. The most amazing thing, though, was that he expected me to sell *him* on the company versus his demonstrating why he was someone worth pursuing. My

> *The most amazing thing was that he expected me to sell him on the company.*

decision was made in the first minute of the interview. It was my easiest interview of the day.

If you want to work at an organization, the message is crystal clear: You have to put in the effort up front to impress them enough so that they will want to talk to you more. First impressions matter greatly, and it's not enough to just avoid a negative first impression. Neutral first impressions at best position you equally with other candidates and at worst put you at the bottom of the list. Why some candidates gamble with first impressions boggles my mind; it is completely within the candidate's control to create that positive first impression. If someone doesn't care enough to make the strongest impression possible, I don't want him as an employee. End of story.

Get prepared for that interview, and use the following ideas to help you:

- **Do your organization research.** In today's Internet culture, learning about almost any organization is only a few mouse clicks away. Learn about what the organization sells, how many employees they have, their sales and net profit, their key business challenges. The more you know and the more you can *show* you know, the more you're likely to impress your interviewer.

- **Talk to someone who already works at your potential employer.** Got a friend, relative, or acquaintance who works at the organization? Buy him a cup of coffee and learn about his experience with the organization. You may learn things that either confirm the organization is a good fit for you or that cause you not to want to work there.

- **Ask someone to mock-interview you.** Ask a friend, colleague, or family member with experience in interviewing to run you through a mock interview. The goal isn't to be gentle and lob softball questions at you. Your mock interviewer should ask you the difficult questions and get you out of your comfort zone. The better you can respond to the difficult questions in a mock interview, the better you'll do when the real interview comes along.

- **Learn as much as you can about the job.** Ask your contact at the company for a job description prior to the interview. Talk to others who work at the company. Talk to someone with a similar job at a different company. Any little bit of information you can dig up will help.

- **Learn about your interviewer.** Find out the name of the person or persons who will be interviewing you. Has she written any books? Has she published any articles? Is she doing a speech or presentation somewhere that you can attend? Do you know someone who might know the person? Does the interviewer have information either on the organization's website or her own website? You may learn about a common interest or idea that could help you establish a connection with your interviewer.

- **Dress the part.** For Pete's sake, dress like you want a job. Make sure your shoes are shined, your shirt or blouse is pressed, and your hair is combed. Even in today's casual environment, most employers expect interviewees to dress business formal. I've never chosen not to hire someone because he overdressed for an interview, but I've declined quite a few who looked like they just crawled out of bed.

■ **Be on time.** 'Nuff said.

If someone doesn't care enough to make the strongest impression possible, I don't want him as an employee.

I can't think of a single instance in my experience where someone was eliminated from a job search because he was too prepared for the interview. Do your homework, prepare for the tough questions, and dress up for the interview, and you'll leave a positive impression on your interviewer. It may not guarantee you a job, but it certainly won't hurt your chances, either.

TRUTH 37

CRITICAL THINKING DRILLS INFLUENCE HIRING DECISIONS

If you had to build a 150-story building, how would you go about it?

How many gas stations are there in the U.S.?

How would you test a toaster?

How would you design a coffeemaker for an automobile?

You've probably heard of some of these legendary interview questions being asked at many high-tech companies—questions that baffle an interviewee, such as how manhole covers possibly relate to a job as a developer, marketing manager, or financial controller. On the surface, these seem like highly peculiar and illogical questions for an interviewer to be asking. However, rather than focusing on the answer, the interviewer is examining the thought process the interviewee uses to come up with the answer.

What is an interviewer looking for when asking how you would design a coffeemaker for an automobile? When I do interviews, I look for several things:

- **Creativity.** What unique and innovative ideas you apply to a problem.

- **Critical thinking.** How quickly you think on your feet and what assumptions you make to analyze problems and develop solution alternatives.

- **Grace under pressure.** How you respond when put under pressure.

In one interview I conducted, the interviewee had a good resume and did great with answering technical questions. I was feeling pretty good about the interviewee and was leaning toward hiring him. Then I asked him how he would build a 150-story building. This is where things fell apart. He simply couldn't show critical thinking or creativity in his thought process, and he stammered through an answer. I ended up declining the candidate because, while I thought he had the technical skills to do the job, he didn't demonstrate some of the core attributes my company looked for in its employees.

When you're being interviewed, here are some techniques to keep in mind when faced with "manhole cover" questions:

- **Verbalize your thought process.** These types of questions are meant to assess your thought process. Don't be afraid to verbalize your thoughts so that your interviewer can follow how you think through problems. You won't get any points for working something out in your head and then blurting out an answer.

- **Allow your creativity to show through.** From my perspective, the more creative and innovative the thought process and answer, the more I am impressed with an interviewee. Don't be afraid to color outside the lines on your answer.

- **Feel free to sketch something out.** Don't be afraid to step up to a whiteboard or pull out a sheet of paper and sketch something out. Again, how you think through problems is the most important thing to demonstrate, so if sketching something helps your thought process, by all means do so.

> *The more creative and innovative the thought process and answer, the more I am impressed with an interviewee.*

- **Use assumptions to estimate your answer.** Interviewers like to see how you use assumptions to estimate an answer. For instance, one way to answer the question about how many gas stations there are in the U.S. would be to take the number of people in the U.S. and then estimate the number of people per gas station.

- **Stay concise and avoid babbling.** Verbalizing your thought process is good, but try to keep things concise and avoid babbling or random verbalizing. If you need to stop for a few seconds to collect your thoughts, do so.

- **Don't panic.** If you get one of these questions, don't panic. Take a deep breath, think about it for a few seconds, and have fun with your answer. Yes, you're being interviewed for a job you'd really like, but in the grand scheme of things, it's just a job. Stay calm and let your creative juices flow.

■ **Don't insult the interviewer.** During one interview, I asked an interviewee how he would go about testing a toaster. The interviewee asked what relevance that had to the job and told me it was a dumb question. His response told me everything I needed to know and made my hiring decision very easy. Insulting the interviewer only demonstrates arrogance on your part. Don't do it.

Oddball questions are intended to see how you think, how creative you are, and how you respond under pressure.

Expect that you'll be asked oddball questions. Remember that they are intended to see how you think, how creative you are, and how you respond under pressure. Just stay calm, verbalize your thought process, show some creativity, and have fun with your answer. You'll get your point across to your interviewer and will make a positive impression that can mean the difference between being hired and being passed over.

TRUTH 38

LIE ABOUT YOUR CREDENTIALS, KILL YOUR CAREER

Notre Dame football coach George O'Leary resigned five days after being hired, admitting he lied about his academic and athletic background. O'Leary claimed to have a master's degree in education and to have played college football for three years, but checks into his background showed these claims weren't true.

Veritas CFO Kenneth Lonchar was fired because he claimed he had a master of business administration from Stanford University. Further research showed that he did not hold an MBA from any school. Ironically, "Veritas" in Latin means "truth."

Joseph Ellis, a Pulitzer Prize–winning historian, was suspended for a year from Mount Holyoke College for lying about serving in the Vietnam War.

Each of these examples, while high-profile and extreme, all fell from the same tree: people lying on their resumes to help influence an employer to hire them. Aside from the fact that each of these cases resulted in job loss or suspension, they also all endured the humiliation of being publicly labeled a liar. Not the best way to be remembered.

Resumes are meant to inform, impress, and inspire a potential employer to talk to you. Most employers spend only about 20 seconds looking at each resume they receive. Even worse, most employers view the information contained on resumes as a way to weed out applicants.[8] Putting your best foot forward to present a concise, compelling case for why you should be hired is crucial to getting invited to the party.

Throughout my career I've interviewed hundreds of candidates for a wide variety of jobs. Many of the candidates I've interviewed were upstanding, honest, and candid and went on to have successful careers at my company. Of those who didn't get hired, a number lost out because of boastful claims made on their resumes that they were unable to substantiate during the interview process. As an interviewer, I intentionally focused on claims that were exceptional to understand how they did it and to see if the claim was authentic or bogus. Authentic claims went a long way toward recommending a "hire" decision; bogus claims got an automatic "no hire" without further consideration.

Most employers spend only about 20 seconds looking at each resume they receive.

Let me put this as plainly as I can: **Lies about your credentials can permanently kill your career.** Putting bogus, or even mildly aggressive, claims on your resume can hurt you in a couple of ways. The first question that arises pertains to competence. Bogus claims will cause a potential employer to question whether you possess the skills required to perform the job. The second question, which is far more important for me, pertains to integrity. If a candidate is willing to stretch the truth on his or her resume, what else is he or she not being truthful about? Having the interviewer question your integrity is pretty much your one-way ticket home.

The lesson learned here is simple: Any lie, even the littlest white lie, has no place on a resume and will come back to bite you. Assume that every word on your resume will be checked, questioned, and scrutinized during an interview and verification. Be able to substantiate facts, metrics, and credentials with backup information, and provide references where necessary.

Having said all this, do your best to sell yourself on your resume, and dazzle prospective employers with your accomplishments, credentials, and experience. Wow them during your 20 seconds of fame. Just make sure that what they see is you and not some figment of your imagination.

TRUTH 39

BABBLING IS FOR BABIES, NOT INTERVIEWS

Some years back I was interviewing candidates for a financial analyst position. One of my interviews was with a gentleman who was already a company employee but was looking for a new job within the company. I started the interview by asking, "What interests you about this job?" The fellow started his response but then launched into tangents about his family, prior jobs, and personal interests. About 5 minutes into the interview I'd already decided not to hire the guy, but I was intrigued by his verbal meandering. I decided to let him keep going just to see where he would end up. He finally stopped talking after half an hour. My next question to him was, "Do you realize you talked nonstop for 30 minutes?" Before he could launch into another wandering discourse, I thanked him for stopping by and told him I didn't think he was right for the job.

My next question to him was, "Do you realize you talked nonstop for 30 minutes?"

He very well might have had the technical and business skills needed to do the job, but because he babbled on and on without clarity of thought, he was eliminated.

The demonstration of clear, concise thoughts through responses to interview questions is a major factor for your interviewer in deciding whether to hire you. When you respond to questions, your interviewer is not only listening to your answers but also imagining you talking with colleagues, suppliers, customers, or executives. If you, as an interviewee, can't respond with crisp, concise, thoughtful answers during an interview, imagine how you would come off in a major customer presentation. You may have some insightful things to say, but if they get lost in long, meandering responses, you'll seal your fate as a declined candidate.

The next time you interview for a job, keep the following things in mind:

- **Target your responses around a key message.** When asked a question, formulate your response around a key message or a series of key messages. State your key message first, and then provide a couple of sentences that support it. Know what your key message is before you start talking, or your response will meander.

- **Watch the interviewer for frustration.** Look for cues that the interviewer is impatient, confused, or bored. The best interviews I've done have been where an interviewee captured my interest by stating a key message and then we just talked. Look to capture the interviewer's interest. If he or she looks disinterested, wrap up your point and stop talking.

- **Maintain eye contact with the interviewer.** Maintaining eye contact helps you stick to your key message, because you won't get distracted. Eye contact also demonstrates conviction and confidence. Wandering eyes feel evasive and can contribute to babbling.

- **Take a breath before you respond.** Let the interviewer finish his question before you start responding. Take a second after the question, get your key message in your head, and then start your answer. Being too eager to answer the question will contribute to drifting from your key message and will brand you as rude.

- **Don't argue with yourself.** Don't play point/counterpoint with yourself. When asked a question, formulate your key message and take a stand in your response. It's OK to briefly identify the other side of an argument, but make sure you state a key message and don't give the perception that you are indecisive.

- **Provide context to your answers.** Don't just give yes-or-no-type answers without providing a bit of context behind the responses. The interviewer wants to know not only what your answer is, but also something about why you think the way you do. Be cautious about drifting on and on with your answer; make a couple of statements that support your key message, and then clam up.

- **Ask your interviewer for feedback.** At the end of the interview, consider asking the interviewer to give you some feedback on how he thinks the interview went. Specifically, ask about the quality and conciseness of your responses. Just be careful not to get into an argument about the interviewer's feedback; listen politely, and then thank him for the feedback. Don't create a negative impression with the interviewer by arguing or getting defensive over any feedback you receive.

It's easy when nervous or excited to babble on and on and lose focus in your responses to questions. Formulate key messages, maintain eye contact, watch your interviewer, and take a stand with your responses. You'll better engage your interviewer, captivate his or her interest, and help secure the job you want.

TRUTH 40

IMPRESS FIRST, AND THEN TALK COMPENSATION

As a manager I've been amused by the different approaches some interviewees have taken over the years. There are a couple of interviews that stand out as Academy Award contenders for Best Arrogant Performance.

Performance number one features an inexperienced, newly degreed interviewee who I'll call "Pug." Pug showed up for the interview on time, was well dressed, and looked well prepared for the interview. I opened the interview with a simple greeting, offered Pug something to drink, and let him know what would happen in the interview. Before I could get my first question out, Pug informed me of his salary expectations and told me

Before I could get my first question out, he informed me of his salary expectations.

that there were other companies willing to meet his expectations. His expectations were about two times what we typically paid newly degreed candidates, and I knew we would never be able to pay Pug what he was looking for. I decided to acknowledge that

Pug had a salary expectation and basically went through the motions for the rest of the interview. I had made my "decline" decision within the first few minutes of the interview.

Performance number two features a very experienced and qualified candidate I'll call "Kip." Kip had an extensive resume with experience that would be valuable to me and showed a lot of promise. I wasn't completely sold on Kip, so I was looking forward to our interview. Throughout the interview, his tone was one of "you have to sell me on why I should work for you," and he let me know that it would take "a lot of money" to lure him away from his current job. I was very disappointed, because someone I initially felt had promise turned into an arrogant mercenary looking to sell his services to the highest bidder. Kip ended up staying at his current employer and not coming to work with me.

Both performances had a common thread running through them. They both introduced compensation into the discussion before I had a chance to decide if I wanted them as employees. Now, don't get me wrong—compensation is a big component of why we work; the mortgage needs to be paid, the kids need braces, and the government wants its cut. You need to ensure that you are compensated fairly for the work you do. However, there is an appropriate time to discuss compensation, and that is after the employer has decided he or she wants you and you've decided you want to be an employee. Before we get too deep into this, I'll assume that you've done some basic homework on the job and that you're not expecting to make $100,000 a year for a job that pays $30,000. If there's that large of a gap, either realign your expectations or don't go forward with the interviewing process.

Assuming that there is a match in compensation expectations, your priorities in the interviewing process need to start with nailing the qualifications. Most successful advertising campaigns don't show you the price of the product first and then explain the value it provides. They get you to see how the product will meet one of your needs, and then they tell you how much it costs (and what a good deal it is for you!). Your interviewing strategy is no different; you want to show how you meet a need and how you can solve a prospective employer's problem before discussing compensation. Once an employer understands your qualification and envisions your value to his company, he can better focus on compensation.

Want some ideas on how to nail the qualifications first? Check these out:

- **Show the interviewer you want the job.** Follow the preparation advice outlined in Truth 36. Ask good questions that demonstrate your interest in the job. Be interested, and let the interviewer see it. Don't worry that you're losing negotiating leverage because you're showing interest. You want him or her to get excited about the prospects of your doing the job.

- **Don't play hard to get.** Showing disinterest or indifference about the job to get the prospective employer to woo you away from your current job is just bad form. More often than not, the prospective employer will walk away rather than play your game. Come off like a prima donna and it may backfire on you, and you'll miss out on a job you really wanted.

- **Find a problem and offer to help solve it.** During your interview, draw out a real-life problem the prospective employer is experiencing, and offer to do a bit of research and write up some things that could be done to solve the problem. This will make a great impression. If the interviewer accepts your offer, burn the midnight oil if necessary to get your thoughts down, and send them to the interviewer within 24 hours of your interview. The couple of times interviewees have done this with me, I was impressed not only by the content they provided but also by their initiative and responsiveness. Both interviewees ultimately ended up as employees.

- **Talk as if you already have the job.** I like it when interviewees use "we" language during an interview. I don't view it as presumptuous; I view it as the interviewee wanting to be part of a team and dig in and get things done. Don't be afraid to talk as if you are a company person; your interviewer is trying to assess your fit within the company, so show him or her.

Establish yourself as a viable and qualified candidate prior to negotiating compensation. Your best opportunity to ensure a fair compensation package is to first get the interviewer to truly want you through showcasing your skills, showing initiative, and demonstrating your desire to be an employee. Get him or her to love you first, and then talk compensation.

> *Get the interviewer to love you first, and then talk compensation.*

PART IX

THE TRUTH ABOUT GIVING FEEDBACK

TRUTH 41

LATE FEEDBACK IS JUST AS BAD AS
NO FEEDBACK AT ALL

Earlier in my career I had a very nice, kind, competent manager who I genuinely liked and enjoyed working for. He was very good at managing projects, working with clients, and delivering results. We did a number of projects together and had an overall good working relationship. He did have one blind spot, though: He was horrendous about giving timely feedback. Unfortunately, I found this out the hard way.

Our first project went very well. We worked hard, delivered on time, and really pleased the client. I got a great performance evaluation from my manager and was thrilled with his comments. Our second project didn't go as well. I did several things wrong on the project that affected the work of several of my colleagues. Unfortunately, I didn't find out about these things until my next performance evaluation, which was three months after the incidents happened. The discussion during my performance evaluation was frustrating because not only was the feedback not timely, but the facts and details were sketchy since so much time had passed. While I did learn something from the discussion, the feedback was not nearly as helpful as it could have been if it were given to me immediately after the event occurred.

Giving feedback. Sometimes it goes well, but other times it is like volunteering to walk into the lion's den. When feedback sessions go well, both sender and recipient walk away from the discussion wiser about how to deal with a situation differently and relieved that the feedback session went well. On the other hand, bad feedback sessions leave at least one if not both sides hurt, angry, and less trusting of each other.

Valid, helpful, and constructive feedback can help a recipient change his or her behavior and improve on any deficiencies he or she may have. Delivering the feedback either late or not at all just isn't helpful to the recipient. It's even worse if the sender stores the feedback in a closet full of skeletons and later clobbers the recipient with the feedback at a time advantageous to the sender. Now, the feedback isn't only late, it's used as a weapon. You may ultimately have a happy ending, but you're likely to have a lot of hurt feelings and bad blood along the way.

If you have valid, helpful, constructive feedback to give, don't procrastinate or store it away for future use. Follow these guidelines:

- **Be timely.** Providing feedback as close to the event as possible is always the best approach, because the event is fresh in minds and can be related to more easily. However, make sure you're not providing feedback out of emotion and positioning yourself for an emotional argument. Go out for a walk or sleep on it first, and then give the feedback. Try not to wait longer than a day or so, because the feedback's effectiveness decreases the longer you wait.

- **Get some coaching if necessary before giving feedback.** Consider running your feedback by a trusted colleague, friend, or spouse before giving it to the recipient. Ensure that you don't make it a gripe session or an attempt to get support for your position. Heed your coach's feedback and incorporate it into the feedback for your recipient. Another benefit of using a coach is that it helps build your confidence in delivering the feedback and enforces some accountability on you to do it.

- **Don't offer feedback if your emotions aren't in check.** If you can't seem to get over any anger or frustration, don't offer the feedback, even if a couple of days have passed. If you can't be factual and unemotional about your feedback, it won't come across as feedback; it will sound more like you're picking on the recipient. Get over your emotions and then give the feedback.

If you have valid, constructive, helpful feedback to offer, do it sooner rather than later. Hold off if you're angry, frustrated, or upset until you calm down and can offer feedback constructively. Offering feedback too late or with too much emotion reduces its effectiveness and can unnecessarily ruffle feathers.

Offering feedback too late or with too much emotion reduces its effectiveness.

TRUTH 42

ENVIRONMENT MATTERS

Early in my career I learned many of my lessons the hard way; I had to make my own mistakes as opposed to learning from others. Given that, I had the opportunity to be on the receiving end of many feedback sessions. Some of them went well, but others didn't. One manager was particularly good about delivering feedback. He was very factual, unemotional, and empathetic. The thing I remember most, though, was how he ensured the setting was comfortable. Whenever we would have feedback discussions, we would sit at a table in his office. The door was closed, the phone was turned off, and there were no other distractions. I felt, even though I was getting some hard feedback on things I needed to improve, that he was making every effort to deliver the message in as comfortable a setting as possible. I was very impressed with this aspect of how he delivered feedback, and the messages delivered have stuck with me for years.

In all my feedback sessions, I never encountered anyone who overtly made the session uncomfortable. I never endured a bright spotlight with "Where were you on the night of the 14th?" questions thrown at me. I have, though, been through feedback sessions where the environment wasn't uncomfortable, but there wasn't an effort to make things comfortable either. I'm in no way advocating that extraordinary measures need be taken to conduct a feedback session, but anything you can do to reduce some of the angst will better ensure that the messaging is clear and that the feedback is better accepted.

> *I was impressed by how he delivered feedback, and the messages delivered have stuck with me for years.*

After all, it's about getting the feedback message across, not how much you make the recipient sweat in the process.

Next time you are delivering feedback, consider the following to better ensure a more conducive environment:

- **Minimize distractions.** Turn off the ringer on your phone (this goes for cell phones too). Make sure your computer screen is out of sight so that an e-mail or instant message won't distract you. Go to a quiet place where you and the other person can sit and talk without any extraneous noise or distraction. Giving feedback is tough enough without having to compete with any attention diversions.

- **Don't sit behind your desk.** Sitting behind your desk creates a perception of power on your part and can cause your feedback session to become one of power rather than constructive advice. Putting yourself in a position of power puts the recipient on guard and reduces the likelihood that your feedback will be accepted. Sit at a table, go to the person's office, or go somewhere else. Just make sure you don't go somewhere where distractions are likely to affect your discussion.

■ **Talk face to face if at all possible.** You're likely to get better results if you can discuss face to face and not only hear verbal reactions but see nonverbal reactions, such as crossed arms (which signify an unwillingness to cooperate) or facial expressions. I've tried to give feedback through e-mail or over the phone and have not been nearly as successful as giving it face to face. If you can talk face to face, do it.

Giving feedback is tough enough; you don't need environmental issues detracting from your message and making a difficult situation even more difficult. Avoid distractions, make the environment as comfortable for the recipient as you can, and give the feedback face to face. You'll get your point across better, and your recipient will appreciate your effort.

TRUTH 43

FOCUS ON THE BEHAVIOR, NOT THE PERSON

One of my favorite movies is *Back to the Future*. Marty McFly is a teenager who travels from 1985 back to 1955 in a quirky professor's time machine built out of a stainless-steel DeLorean automobile. Marty's high school teacher, Mr. Strickland, loves to say to Marty, "You're a slacker, McFly, just like your old man." Mr. Strickland never cites what Marty's "slacker" behaviors are or how to turn things around. He calls him a slacker because he thinks Marty's father, George McFly, was a slacker. Mr. Strickland is king of providing feedback that focuses on the person, not the behavior.

True, this example is Hollywood giving outrageous character attributes to an outrageous movie character in order to embellish a story line. However, most of us have, at some point in our lives, encountered someone who attacked us as a person rather than focusing on our behaviors. Maybe it was a parent who referred to you as an idiot, school kids who called you fat, or an employer who labeled you as lazy. The feedback was not provided as constructive and meant to help you; it was destructive, expressed out of anger or disappointment, and meant to hurt you. Maybe it worked in some cases, like causing the guy who was called fat enough times to hit the gym and lose four belt notches. On the other hand, it just might have caused him to further climb into a shell and get consolation from more food. My general view here is this: Focusing feedback on the person tends to be destructive and is meant to hurt; focusing feedback on the behavior tends to be constructive and is meant to help.

Focus on the behavior and not the person by employing some of these techniques:

- **Jot down the behaviors you want to give feedback on ahead of time.** Know the specific situation and behaviors that raised your eyebrows, and write them down ahead of time. Ensure that the behaviors are factual and easily understandable. If you feel you may not be able to judge the emotional content of the feedback, ask a colleague to review whether your feedback is factually driven and not emotionally charged.

- **If something was done well, say so.** If your recipient did something well, start your feedback session with the things that were done well. Don't worry that you may be dampening the effect of the constructive feedback because you also gave positive feedback. Mixing positive and constructive feedback tells the recipient you are being objective and balanced and makes your feedback more effective.

- **Avoid emotional attacks.** Statements like "You idiot!" or "Your ideas are stupid!" are very general, have no constructive value, and don't belong in a feedback session (or anywhere else, for that matter). Your feedback should focus on fact and some unemotional assessment, such as "The joke you told in the meeting today could have been offensive to some of the attendees."

- **Let them know how the behavior affected you or others.** Suppose you are giving feedback to your recipient on his inability to meet deadlines. The feedback could be "You have not met the last three deadlines assigned to you. Your colleagues need to take on additional work that was to be assigned to you because you are not meeting assigned deadlines." Helping the recipient understand the impact of his behavior helps him understand the need to change.

- **Establish an understanding on desired behavior.** Clearly outline for the recipient what behavior is desired. Using the preceding deadline example, the desired behavior would be as follows: "The team needs you to meet each deadline given to you to keep the project on schedule." Even though this may seem unnecessary at times, you're better off ensuring that the desired behavior is clear to the recipient and that he agrees to it.

Feedback doesn't give you license to attack a person's character, ethics, or intelligence. Feedback should focus on specific behaviors and ensure that you and the recipient have a clear understanding of what the behavior was, how it impacted you and others, and what the desired behavior is moving forward. Success here is where the recipient changes

Feedback doesn't give you license to attack a person's character, ethics, or intelligence. It should focus on specific behaviors.

his or her behavior as a result of the feedback and improves as a person. Help the recipient and make the feedback clear, constructive, and actionable.

TRUTH 44

SOMETIMES IT'S BEST NOT TO OFFER YOUR FEEDBACK

Despite my very best intentions, I have encountered some people throughout my life who simply are not interested in and do not want my feedback. I would spend a lot of time writing down behaviors, focusing on how I thought others perceived their behavior, and my desired changes to their behavior. I would focus on facts and keep things as unemotional as possible during the feedback session. Even though I did all the right things, my feedback sessions would go bust.

In looking at what went wrong in my failed feedback sessions, I was able to narrow it down to several key factors:

- My relationship with the recipient wasn't trusting to a point where I could provide feedback safely.
- My perspective on the situation was wrong, and I provided feedback inappropriately.
- I hadn't learned how to give good, constructive, empathetic feedback.

When I was a young manager, I had a very experienced administrative assistant who worked with me. She was very competent in her job and did everything I needed very well.

One thing that bothered me, though, was her workstation, with its numerous stacks of paper all around. I, in my naivete, couldn't understand how she could get things done with all that clutter, so I suggested that she clean up her workstation to be more effective. Bad move. She got pretty ticked with me and asked whether her workstation affected her ability to do her job. She was dead right, and it took me a long time to rebuild my relationship with her. My feedback was not steeped in fact; it was based on my perception of what I thought was right. Painful lesson.

Before you offer feedback, think about the following things and then decide:

- **You already have a strained relationship with the recipient.** As desperately as you may be to provide feedback to a recipient, you may not have a trusting relationship built with the recipient to provide effective feedback. If you don't have that trusting relationship, clam up on the feedback. If you're not sure, ask a colleague who knows both you and the recipient, and get his or her opinion.

If you don't have a trusting relationship with the recipient, clam up on the feedback.

- **You're unsure of the facts.** You may feel compelled to offer feedback, but if the facts are sketchy, do your homework first. You may find that the feedback is legitimate, but you may also find that the feedback is unwarranted because the facts don't support the need for feedback. Be clear on the facts before you formulate your feedback.

- **You're not in an authoritative position to offer the feedback.** A number of years back I offered some feedback to a colleague on his attitude in team meetings. He in no uncertain terms told me to stick it where the sun doesn't shine and said that because I was just a peer he wasn't willing to listen. My error was that I offered feedback to a colleague who didn't see it as my place to do so because I wasn't in an authoritative position and didn't have a good enough relationship with him to offer peer feedback.

- **You've been told that you don't give good feedback.** You may feel compelled to offer feedback, but if you've been told that you aren't effective at offering constructive feedback, resist the urge. Work on your feedback-giving skills with a colleague or friend in "practice sessions" using some of the techniques I've highlighted in this book.

Sometimes the best feedback you can provide is no feedback at all. If your feedback will only add fuel to the fire because of strained relationships, unclear facts, or your inability to deliver effective feedback, hold your tongue and let someone else do it. You'll save yourself and your recipient a lot of stress and will keep from further deteriorating a relationship.

TRUTH 45

BE OPEN TO FEEDBACK, AND THEN DECIDE HOW TO USE IT

In writing this book I went through an extensive feedback process. After I wrote the chapters, my wife reviewed them, making grammatical corrections and suggesting changes to content. Then I sent each chapter to a group of reviewers, who assessed the chapter's applicability, practicality, and appeal. Then I sent it to a reviewer at my publisher who suggested still more changes. Then editors reviewed the manuscript and suggested wording and other changes. Once the book is published, the real feedback begins. Book reviewers, readers, and journalists all give their opinions on the book. It's feedback with a capital "F."

I appreciated the feedback I received on this book. My reviewers were prompt, reliable, and, most importantly, *honest*. They didn't tell me what I wanted to hear; they told me what they thought and helped me make the book better. The feedback process worked very well for me.

This situation is an example of solicited feedback. I asked a specific group for specific feedback and expected them to give me honest, direct input on my work product. I was prepared for the feedback and was expecting it. No problem.

Unsolicited feedback, though, can be a bit trickier. Typically you're unprepared for the feedback and may not think you need it. Acknowledging feedback without getting defensive also is difficult. Keep two things in mind in this situation. The first is that someone is giving you feedback to help you, not hurt you. A friend, colleague, or family member wants to see a change for the better in something you're doing. This is why he or she offers feedback. The motive is generally pure, not divisive.

Now, there are those malicious few who give feedback just to break you down and hurt you; I'm not talking about those jerks. You can typically tell a malicious offender because he usually is unwilling to offer constructive advice as part of the feedback; his motivation is just to rip you apart. That's not the feedback I'm talking about; that's trash talk.

The second thing to keep in mind is that you control what you do with the feedback. A well-meaning person may offer some feedback without having a full understanding of what you're doing, so you still need to decide what to implement.

What are some things to do when you're offered feedback? Look at doing the following:

■ **Acknowledge the feedback.** Most likely, someone is offering feedback to help you. Acknowledge the feedback and appreciate that he or she at least took the time to give you some input. Acknowledgement doesn't mean you'll necessarily take action—merely that you'll consider it.

■ **Seek clarification if the feedback is vague.** If someone is trying to offer feedback but is being vague or general, seek clarification. Do this to truly understand someone's perspective and not to try to corner him or make him justify his position. If his feedback is still vague, acknowledge it and move on.

- **Ask for advice on how to implement the feedback.** Chances are, your colleague offering feedback also has opinions on how to implement changes. Hear her out; there may be a couple of good ideas you can use. If not, you're no worse off than before the feedback.

- **Look for trends.** If one person gives you feedback, you can use your judgment in either considering it or not. However, if you hear the same feedback from a number of people, it is probably something you should take more seriously. You still control what you accept and how you accept it, but if you hear the same feedback a number of times from different people, that's a pretty strong indication that you should accept the feedback.

- **Don't get defensive.** Try your best not to take the feedback personally. Your colleague may not be the best at giving feedback, and he or she may really bungle it when delivering the message. By and large, your colleague is just trying to help. Acknowledge the feedback and consider using it later.

Try not to take feedback personally.

Recognize that your colleague wants to help in giving feedback, get clarification if needed, don't get defensive, and decide if you want to implement the feedback. Do look for trends in feedback, though. If a number of people tell you the same thing, you should more strongly consider implementing the feedback.

PART X

THE TRUTH ABOUT BEING A GOOD LISTENER

TRUTH 46

LISTENING MEANS LETTING THEM TALK

In my earlier years I viewed myself as a very good listener. In school I listened to my teachers, followed directions well, and got good grades. I was able to listen to my bosses and follow their directions well. I was raised to view listening as following directions and doing what others in authority told me to do. I was pretty good at it. Then one event happened that changed my listening journey forever: marriage.

The one event that changed my listening journey forever was marriage.

My wife, Patty, is the best wife a husband could have. She's supportive, helpful, and attentive to both my needs and those of our kids. What I didn't know about her, and had to learn, was that we have different listening styles. I am a problem solver, so if someone brings a problem to me, by golly I try to solve it. I am much more interested in the destination (the resolution to the problem) as opposed to the journey (the things that lead up to solving the problem). Patty, on the other hand, is interested in the destination, but the journey is also important to her. When she brings up a problem to me, she doesn't necessarily want me to plunge in and solve it for her. She wants me to listen to the details, her feelings about the problem, and whatever else she feels is important to provide context to the problem. She welcomes my input into helping her solve the problem, but I have to allow some of the journey to happen before I jump to the destination. As I thought about this in relation to other areas of my life, I started to change my thinking about listening. To be a good listener, you have to let the other person talk.

Think about that for a minute. To be a good listener, you have to let the other person talk. Now there's a revelation! But when you peel back the onion, being a good listener doesn't equate to being efficient, but to being effective. An efficient listener may be able to hear a problem, diagnose it, and come up with solutions in record time. But if others don't process as quickly or don't feel ownership of the solution, the solution may not get implemented because it was your idea, not theirs.

Provide an open climate to let them talk by doing the following:

- **Provide a comfortable environment.** You want to provide an environment where your colleague feels as if you, the receiver, are wholly dedicated to listening to him or her. Sit at a table rather than behind your desk, and close the door. Your colleague should feel as if he or she is the most important person on your calendar and that nothing will interrupt your discussion.

- **Help articulate the problem.** Problem articulation may be difficult, particularly if your colleague is angry, distraught, or frustrated. If she isn't clear on the problem, help her articulate exactly what problem needs to be solved. It's very important that you don't show impatience or frustration with your colleague, since it may cause her to withdraw and not want to share openly. Have some patience as you help your colleague get clarity on her problem.

- **Assist with problem solving; don't plunge in and do it yourself.** If you're like me, you may want to tell the person what he needs to do to solve the problem. Resist the urge. A large part of what you're doing is helping the person internalize his problem, take ownership of it, and devise and own a solution that addresses the problem. If you blurt out a solution, your colleague may go off and execute tasks, but it is *your* solution that will be executed, not his. Even if he comes up with the exact same solution, you need to let him go through some discovery and devise his own solution.

- **Be empathetic.** Be helpful, patient, and interested in the conversation. If you're wrestling with tough issues on your own, or you have a looming deadline that is occupying your mind that keeps you from focusing on your colleague, defer your discussion. It's better to put off a discussion for a couple of days until you can truly help the person than to come across as impatient or distracted because you have your own fish to fry.

Let the person talk. Create a comfortable environment where he feels free to open up. Help articulate the problem, but don't plunge in and solve it for him. Just make sure that you are prepared for the discussion by not having your own issues or deadlines that will distract you.

TRUTH 47

DON'T HANG OUT A THERAPIST SHINGLE
UNLESS YOU'RE A THERAPIST

Alex was one of the kindest, most empathetic people you could meet. She had a true gift for listening to others' problems and helping them with issues. Anytime someone wanted to talk to Alex about anything, she would drop what she was doing and provide an empathetic ear. She was viewed as a wonderful friend by many.

Alex joined an organization as a customer service representative. Her open, honest, and empathetic approach was refreshing to customers, and she received several positive comments on her abilities. As she got to know her coworkers, they quickly recognized her gift of listening, and many took the opportunity to talk to her. Alex was very responsive to her coworkers and would drop everything whenever someone wanted to talk with her. As time progressed, her work performance deteriorated as she spent more and more time listening to and helping her coworkers. When a downturn in business hit and the organization needed to reduce its workforce, Alex was one of the first people to be laid off even though she was well liked and respected by her coworkers. She placed such a high value on listening to others and helping them

She placed such a high value on listening to and helping others that her work performance suffered.

with their problems that her work performance suffered and ultimately cost her a job.

Being a warm, empathetic listener is a valuable skill. I've always had great joy when I was able to listen to someone's issues and help him or her with a difficult problem. Despite the amount of joy I get in helping others, I am not a trained therapist and have never had a job where listening and helping others with problems that didn't relate to my job were my primary responsibilities. Over the years I've had to learn to balance how much time and energy I dedicate to listening to others' issues with my ability to help them and the amount of time I can give them. Being a good listener is a wonderful thing, but doing it to either your own or the other person's detriment isn't good.

In my experience I've zeroed in on a few helpful tips for balancing your listening. The first thing is to prioritize your job responsibilities with the need to listen to others. If you are a manager of people, one of your implied responsibilities is to help the team members in your organization when they are dealing with a difficult issue. Making time to help them is important not only to your team member, but also to the health of your organization. If the person needing help is a peer, friend, or someone you don't manage, be respectful of your organization and limit discussions to times when you're expected to fulfill your primary job responsibilities. Go out for coffee before work, have lunch, or grab a soda afterward when you're off the clock.

The second thing is to be cautious about dropping everything when someone wants to talk. Sometimes the need for a discussion is urgent enough that other responsibilities need to be deferred. Then again, sometimes the discussion can be deferred without significant consequence. If you can't spare the interruption and the need to talk can wait, ask to defer the discussion to a more convenient time.

The third thing is to be conscious of when an issue is beyond your capabilities to help. If a discussion leads to an area in which you don't have knowledge, or if you see that the other person is potentially in danger, suggest that she talk to someone with more expertise, or help her find someone she can talk to. If she took the time to seek you out as someone to talk with, she likely will take your advice to talk with someone who has greater subject matter expertise.

The fourth thing is to watch how involved you get. The best thing you can offer someone is to provide an empathetic ear and objective advice. Getting too close to an issue whereby you are unable to be objective means you cannot be a voice of reason for the other person. If you find you can't stay objective, remove yourself from the situation and suggest that the person talk with someone who *can* be objective.

Being an empathetic listener can be incredibly helpful to someone. Just make sure you don't become an amateur therapist. Listen and give advice where you can, but be aware of where you need to pull yourself out of a situation or when someone with specific expertise should be utilized.

TRUTH 48

KEEP STRESSFUL MEETINGS FROM SPONTANEOUSLY COMBUSTING

It was late afternoon on a sunny spring day. I was cleaning up a few last items before heading out for the day. Just then, an acquaintance I had met only a week earlier (I'll call him "Phil") knocked on my door, said hello, came into my office, closed the door, and sat down. I was a bit surprised, because I had planned on just saying hello and then hightailing it out of my office. For the next hour and a half, Phil poured out his heart about his job, his marriage, and his financial situation. He shifted between sadness, fear, and anger throughout our discussion. It was obvious that he was experiencing some major problems. I was caught flat-footed because I wasn't prepared to have such an intimate conversation, let alone with someone I had just met. I was also getting very impatient with Phil because he had interrupted my plans. Rather than trying to reschedule the

I wasn't prepared to have such an intimate conversation, let alone with someone I had just met.

discussion, I blurted out that I needed to go and left him with the clear impression that I was perturbed with him. I walked out of my office and headed to my car, leaving Phil still upset in the building.

During my drive home, I reflected on my conversation with Phil and felt more and more horrible with each mile. How could I have been so insensitive? Phil was definitely hurting, and rather than try to reschedule some time with him, I cut him off because he interrupted my time. I blew it big time.

It happens. A discussion with someone gets tense, stressful, or upsetting. I've been in a number of discussions in my career where anger or tears were involved. Sometimes I've been able to handle it well and stay calm, empathetic, and supportive of the other person. Then there are times like my encounter with Phil. My own stress fueled the negative energy in the meeting and, rather than helping the discussion, I contributed to its destruction.

Do your part to keep discussions positive and constructive when the stress level goes up by doing the following:

- **Don't say "Calm down."** Saying this to someone who is already upset or stressed can make matters worse, since the person may view this as a personal attack. You want to calm the person down, but you need to use calm, empathetic statements such as "I can understand how that upset you." This shows that you acknowledge his frustration and empathize with the situation. You may or may not agree with his view; that's OK. Focus on calming him down through your voice and actions versus a command.

- **Take a break.** If the stress level starts getting high, consider taking a quick break to let the other person collect his or her thoughts and to keep your stress level down. Politely excuse yourself, and confirm you'll be back. Leave the room for a few minutes and grab a soda. Come back using a calm and quiet tone, and refocus the conversation to the issue at hand.

- **Keep your emotions in check.** One of you being stressed or upset is bad enough; both of you getting that way is sure to make things worse. Work hard to keep your emotions in check, and take some deep breaths along the way to keep yourself calm. If you feel yourself getting too stressed or upset, and you can't bring yourself down while in the discussion, take a break to collect yourself, and let the other person do the same.

> *My stress fueled the negative energy in the meeting, and I contributed to its destruction.*

- **Reschedule your meeting.** If you're out of time or you can't reach some constructive end with the other person, reschedule your meeting to another time when you'll be able to dedicate more time and things will have calmed down. The next meeting will most likely start more constructively and will be focused and less stressful.

- **Take a few minutes before your next meeting.** If your own stress level was elevated during the meeting, give yourself a few minutes to calm down and relax before starting another meeting. Your next meeting attendees don't deserve to experience any of your wrath because your last meeting stressed you out. Take a quick walk and take a few "cleansing breaths" (if you've gone through Lamaze childbirth classes, you know what I mean) before the next meeting. Your meeting attendees will thank you for it.

Stressful and upsetting discussions are tough. When you find yourself in one of these discussions, use calm tones, be empathetic, and consider taking a break if you see yourself losing control. Also, remember not to take your last meeting's stress into your next meeting. A domino effect of stressful meetings will just make your day tougher and keep you from getting your point across.

PART XI

THE TRUTH ABOUT INFORMAL COMMUNICATIONS

TRUTH 49

INFORMAL DOESN'T MEAN INEFFECTIVE

Earlier in my career I worked on a high-profile project to make some major modifications to our firm's commercial manufacturing software that we sold to clients. Our firm's management assigned a very seasoned, knowledgeable senior manager to oversee the project, who I'll call "Brian." Brian exemplified Management by Walking Around (MBWA).[9] He spent his days walking among the more than 100 employees assigned to the project, taking part in informal conversations about the work being done, what employees saw as some of the problems, and what employees thought should be done about the problems. As one of the managers, I was frustrated by Brian's style of management, because he asked me about some of the things he was learning from my employees. Brian knew exactly the questions to ask, and I found myself fumbling for answers to his questions. At first, my frustration was with Brian's meddling, but eventually my frustration was more with myself, because Brian knew more than I did about the problems on my own projects. The informal interactions he had with my employees gave him a much better idea of what was truly happening than I was able to get through structured interactions.

Let's start by naming some attributes of informal communication. Formal communication tends to be scheduled, have arranged participants, and be governed by an agenda. Informal communication, on the other hand, tends to be unscheduled, have random participants, and is not governed by an agenda. Informal communication can focus on just about any topic, from thoughts on a strategic direction to what you did last weekend.

Since my experience working for Brian, I have learned to better use informal communication to help build relationships with people; better understand the work they do; and get a pulse on how satisfied (or dissatisfied) people are with their jobs, the organization, and me. Informal 5-to-10-minute "bursts" of conversation have become core to my leadership philosophy and have helped me become a better leader and communicator.

I have learned to use informal 5-to-10-minute "bursts" of conversation to become a better leader and communicator.

How can you use information communication channels to better understand others' viewpoints and get your viewpoint across? Consider doing the following:

- **Use informal time to build relationships.** Take a couple minutes to ask about someone's family, hobbies, or personal interests. Does someone have a sick child at home? Take a minute to ask how he or she is doing.

What's important here is to be sincere in your interest or concern. Asking someone "Do you have a dog?" every time you see him or her positions you as shallow and disinterested. If you need to, jot down a couple key facts about each person you work with and take the time to ask about one of the facts when you run into the person at the water cooler.

- **Let someone show you what he's working on.** At times you may drop in on a colleague or employee, and he may ask you to look at something he's working on. Take a couple minutes to give the work a quick look and offer up some thoughts. This is particularly powerful if you are a manager and can say "This is really cool stuff" to an employee. This takes only a couple minutes and can work wonders for your employee's motivation.

- **Let your human side come out.** People like to see a bit of your human side, particularly if you are the boss. If you did something fun with your family last weekend or if you have a personal interest, don't be afraid to show it. Virtually everyone who has worked with me knows that my family and my faith are top priorities in my life. I've carried on a number of very effective conversations with people on topics such as working with an autistic child or staying focused when things get tough at work or home.

> *People like to see a bit of your human side, particularly if you are the boss.*

Discussions like these are great investments and, while they may not directly relate to the work you are doing, they go a long way toward helping someone's overall effectiveness as a person.

■ **Don't overstep your bounds on giving direction.** If you're a manager and someone who is a couple levels down from you asks for your opinion, take care not to usurp the authority of that person's direct manager. Any affirming comments you make can be taken as a directive and can create a problem by confusing direction between you and the person's manager. I've had more than one situation where one of my managers came to me asking why I told so-and-so to make changes to a report. So make sure that, along with any affirming comments, you reinforce that the person should be working with his direct manager.

■ **Watch for receptiveness cues.** You can learn a lot from chit-chat, but if someone has her door closed, doesn't make eye contact with you, doesn't stop what she's doing, or appears preoccupied, take the clue and move on. It's not that she doesn't want to talk to you; she's probably just too busy to talk at that moment. Accept the cue and catch up with her later.

Unstructured, random bursts of interaction can be very powerful in helping you understand what's really going on in an organization and can help you build some great relationships. Watch for receptiveness cues, show interest in the person, and take the opportunity to praise good work. Just don't be shallow or insincere in your interactions; people will see right through you and will label you as "going through the motions" versus truly having an interest in what they are working on.

Don't be shallow or insincere in your interactions; people will see right through you.

TRUTH 50

BEWARE THE DROP-IN

Remember Moe from Truth 12? Not only was he an incessant pontificator, he was also king of the drop-ins. Moe loved to go from cubicle to cubicle and talk about the issue of the day or the stupidity of management. Once Moe sat his behind down in a chair, you were in for at least a 10-minute discussion about whatever was on his mind. Moe was also oblivious to polite "I'm busy" signs such as our continuing to type or reading through documents. Once he got started, it was difficult to end a discussion politely. On more than one occasion I simply had to ask Moe to leave, which he would do after he finished whatever revolutionary point he was making.

Let me be clear that I am not such a structured frump that I come unglued if someone wants to have some unscheduled time with me. I actually enjoy this most of the time. There are times, though, when I have deadlines to hit or am focused on something, and the drop-in distracts my thinking. It's the times where drop-ins distract you that I am focusing on in this chapter.

You usually know who the drop-ins are; they may have a reputation like Moe's, or they may just like immediate answers to their questions. Nonetheless, it is up to you to assess whether you can accommodate the drop-in and how to control the conversation. Regardless of the drop-in's characteristics, you still possess the power to engage in the conversation, defer it, or decline it.

If you can't afford to take the time to talk with the drop-in, consider using some of the following techniques:

- **Don't start discussions you can't stop.** The best way to avert a distraction is not to let it happen in the first place. If you're in deep thought on a problem or working toward a deadline, don't let the drop-in divert your focus. Ask him or her to come back another time. The "quick question" can turn into a 10-minute discussion. If you don't have the time, don't start the discussion.

- **Ask if the issue is urgent.** A drop-in may truly have an urgent issue that he or she needs your guidance or input on. If so, stick to the topic, address the urgent question as quickly as you can, and then end the conversation. Be cautious of "pork barreling," where the drop-in takes advantage of the opportunity to discuss nonurgent issues.

- **Don't be lured by "Got a minute?"** Think back to all the times someone has said "Got a minute?" to you. Did the issue truly take only a minute? In my experience, it is typically more like

> *When someone asks, "Got a minute?", ask yourself, "Do I have 10 minutes?"*

5 to 10 minutes. When someone asks, "Got a minute?", ask yourself, "Do I have 10 minutes?" and then assess whether you can spare the time.

- **Train the drop-in to schedule time with you.** Ask the drop-in to schedule time with you, or offer to schedule the meeting yourself. By doing so, you are letting the drop-in know you value what he has to say, while at the same time averting a distraction. Get him to respect your time by scheduling ahead of time as opposed to interrupting your schedule.

- **Stand up.** If you invite or allow a drop-in to sit down in your office or workspace, you've likely entered into at least a 10-minute discussion. If possible, stand up when talking with a drop-in, which keeps him or her standing. A standing drop-in is likely to leave sooner than a sitting drop-in. Also, if you're standing, it's easier for you to end the discussion and leave to tend to other business.

Being accessible, attentive, and available for others doesn't mean you have to be disrupted by a drop-in. If you can't spare the time, assess the urgency, get the drop-in to schedule time with you, and don't be lured by "Got a minute?" You have work to do too, and you need to control your time, schedule, and accessibility to ensure you get it done.

TRUTH 51

FOCUS ON THE BIG GRAPES
ON THE GRAPEVINE

My manager had just acquired a large organization and was beginning the process of integrating it into the existing organization. Through this integration process, it had leaked out that one of the managers in the new organization would be replaced with one of the managers from the existing organization. About four weeks went by between the leak and the actual announcement. During the four-week period there was a significant amount of stress for both organizations because of the impending management changes and a tremendous amount of grapevine speculation about what would happen. The drop-off in productivity was significant because many were concerned that their projects and work would be put on hold, reprioritized, or canceled. The grapevine fostered a near-paralyzing situation in the

The impending management changes created a tremendous amount of speculation about what would happen.

organization because there were so many unanswered questions about the organization's future.

Ah, grapevines—the human reaction to finishing a partially written script. When people are told only part of a story, they often attempt to complete the story with their own observations and speculation. Grapevines facilitate this script-writing through collaboration with others on potential endings to the script. Sometimes grapevines are a relatively harmless part of life that can't be avoided. Other times, as in the preceding example, a grapevine can create a script that panics or upsets people and can significantly impact someone's ability to get things done. Grapevines sprout small grapes and big grapes.

Small grapes on the grapevine are the small things that people speculate on that don't affect their ability to get things done. Speculation on who is dating whom or why the restaurant down the street closed its doors is relatively harmless and generally doesn't inhibit getting things done. So long as people don't spend all their time sprouting small grapes, these discussions aren't a big deal.

Big grapes, however, are more serious. Reorganizations, acquisitions, or new leadership can generate a tremendous amount of speculation that can affect people's ability to get things done. Big grapes that spin tales of layoffs or reassignments can quickly sprout and create fear, uncertainty, and doubt and grind work to a screeching halt. The big grapes can be a big problem unless steps are taken to help prune them before they have a chance to grow.

What can you do to help prune the big grapes from the grapevine? Take these as food for thought:

- **Avoid telling half a story.** Big announcements that tell only part of a story are sure to sprout big grapes on the grapevine. Announcements such as saying that the company will build a facility in an emerging country, without supplying details on what the facility will be used for, will cause big grapes to sprout instantaneously and will divert attention from getting work done by people who now fear for their jobs. People will fill in the details you leave out with speculation, fear, and worry and then will use the grapevine to sprout more big grapes.

- **Keep need-to-know things need-to-know.** Think about how many times someone has said to you, "Don't tell anyone, but...." Now honestly think about the number of times you took that same information, went to someone else, and said, "Don't tell anyone, but...." Interestingly enough, the "Don't tell anyone, but..." statement serves more as your disclaimer than it does as a warning to another person. By you saying it, you've absolved yourself of responsibility if the other person chooses to tell someone else, because she didn't heed your warning. If you're entrusted with need-to-know information, keep it to need-to-know people only.

- **Move quickly on confidential issues.** The longer a confidential issue stays in the works, the more likely information about the issue is to leak out. Because people want to know the full story, they will stitch story fragments together with big grapes from the grapevine. Move as swiftly as possible on confidential items to avert leaks and to keep big grapes from sprouting.

- **Don't make statements unless you have the facts.** Erroneous or incomplete statements are like sprinkling Miracle-Gro on the grapevine. Juicy information backed up by facts generally is assumed to carry greater credibility and will quickly sprout big grapes. Consequently, management resources get consumed with doing damage control and clarifying facts. If you don't have the facts straight, put a sock in it until you do.

Prevent the big grapes from sprouting. Keep need-to-know information need-to-know, move quickly on confidential issues, keep your mouth shut if you don't have the facts, and avoid announcements that tell only part of a story. Just don't preoccupy yourself with the small grapes; they're generally harmless and not worth worrying about.

TRUTH 52

BE ACCESSIBLE,
NOT OPEN-DOOR

The phrase "I have an open-door policy" was very intriguing to me early in my career. As a younger staff person, I envisioned the day when I could be a supportive, empathetic manager who could respond to any of my employees' needs, questions, and comments whenever they needed me. I imagined people coming to my door (which was open, of course) and asking, "Got a minute?" I would stop what I was doing and talk with the employee, he would thank me for being such an inspirational manager, and then I would go back to my work, just like I never left it. Ah, the naivete.

When I actually became a manager, I shortly thereafter gave my empathetic "I have an open-door policy" speech and was ready to solve problems for anyone who crossed my threshold. However, within a few months of my open-door policy, I saw my productivity drop and my frustration level

Within months of my open-door policy, I saw my productivity drop and my frustration level rise.

rise because I kept getting interrupted by people taking me up on my offer. My open-door policy soon turned into a series of random interruptions that kept me from getting things done. I came to recognize that I needed to be *accessible* to people but that I could control the accessibility through scheduled time. Open-door means *be accessible*, not *come in whenever you want*.

I realize that in some ways I am debunking a philosophy that a lot of people subscribe to. I also don't want to be so regimented in my depiction that you think I never permitted drop-ins. Quite the contrary—I really liked the occasional chat or quick questions at the right times. The "be accessible" policy means that you welcome and encourage people to come talk to you, but as a general rule they should schedule time with you just as the requestor would with any other meeting that happens in your organization. Dropping in whenever the requestor feels like it shouldn't be encouraged, particularly when you're already busy.

Also, "be accessible" doesn't mean you'll see anyone about anything. Depending on your level in the organization and your degree of influence, you can spend the vast majority of your time meeting with people who either want to sell you something or want an audience to air their personal grievances. When you get requests for your time, it's a good idea to ask what the requestor wants from you. You can then assess whether it is appropriate to meet with the requestor or to suggest another person the requestor should contact.

The "be accessible" policy works; it just takes some discipline on your part. Do the following to help the "be accessible" policy work for you:

- **Set the expectations up front.** It's very soft and fuzzy to say "My door is always open," but unless you truly mean it, don't say it. A better expectation to set is "Feel free to schedule some time for us to talk." You still maintain a desire to talk to people, but you also set the expectation that they should find time that is workable for you both.

- **Make it easy to schedule time with you.** I've worked with some managers who intentionally block out their entire schedule for months ahead of time and make it very difficult to schedule time to meet. The rationale I've heard is "If someone really wants to meet with me, they'll get on the phone with my assistant and try to find a time that works." Yeesh—what a power trip. If you're truly so busy that every hour is blocked off for the next several weeks, that's understandable. Just don't intentionally make it difficult for someone to see you.

- **Don't be afraid to ask a drop-in to come back at a scheduled time.** If someone does drop in and you're unable to accommodate him or her at the time, be deliberate about asking him or her to schedule some time or to come back at another time that is better for you. You're still being accessible; you're just deferring the discussion until a more convenient time for both of you.

- **Keep the appointments you make.** Stuff happens, and you need to reschedule appointments at times. Try not to blow off these informal chats too much, or your policy of being accessible turns into a big joke.

Being available to talk with people or help them through their problems is a wonderful thing. Don't feel obligated to post an open-door policy. Let people know you're accessible. Also let them know they should work to schedule time with you so that you can give them your undivided attention. You'll accomplish the same goals as with an open-door policy and will get your own work done to boot.

PART XII

THE TRUTH ABOUT INFLUENCING THOSE WHO DON'T WORK FOR YOU

TRUTH 53

SEVEN ATTRIBUTES TO AVOID IF YOU WANT PEOPLE TO FOLLOW YOU

Getting others to follow you when they don't *have* to follow you is a true test of your leadership abilities. Think back to some of the most venerated leaders in American history: George Washington, Martin Luther King, Abraham Lincoln, Susan B. Anthony. People followed them because they had tremendous clarity of purpose, they could articulate that purpose in terms people could understand and rally behind, and they were willing and able to execute to that purpose. They knew that what they stood for could inspire others to follow their cause.

In looking at leadership qualities, I believe seven major barriers can inhibit managers from becoming true leaders.

Arrogance

Ever known a manager who consistently claimed to know more than the rest of the team? How about one who was unwilling to listen to opposing views? Isn't this just a sign of confidence? What's wrong with that?

Confidence as a manager is crucial since people look to you, particularly when things get tough. When it runs amok and turns to arrogance, the manager disrespects the team. Show respect and have confidence, and you'll do fine. Subtract respect, and you're just an arrogant doofus.

Indecisiveness

You have a meeting on Monday, and management agrees on a course of action. On Tuesday, the manager decides to take a completely different course of action. Thursday the manager goes back to Monday's course of action. The following Monday you're rehashing through the same problem from last Monday. Blech.

Decisiveness means that the manager listens to those around him or her, makes the best decision for the organization that the rest of the team can understand, and sticks to it. While team members may not agree with the decision, they should be able to see the rationale. Decisions without rationale or without listening ultimately frustrate the team and put a target on the manager's back.

Disorganization

We've all known a manager who asks for the same information multiple times, keeps the plan in his or her head versus writing things down, or is so frantic that he or she is on the verge of spontaneously combusting. This disorganization creates unneeded stress and frustration for the team.

The manager needs to have a clear pathway paved for the staff to get from start to completion and must make sure that the ball moves forward every day. Disorganization leads to frustration, which leads to either empathy or anarchy.

Stubbornness

Jennifer was a month behind schedule on a three-month project. She refused to alter the project schedule, insisting that she could make up time by cutting corners and eliminating tasks. Despite the entire project team's telling her they were in deep yogurt, she stubbornly forged ahead. Jennifer ended up never seeing the end of the project because her stubbornness got her removed as the project manager. Talk about your 2-by-4 across the head!

The manager may believe his or her view of reality is the right way to go, but it's imperative that she balance her own perspective with the rest of the team. Decisiveness without listening to the team leads to stubbornness.

Negativism

Years back, one of my peer managers, in his zeal to "manage expectations," consistently discussed his projects in a negative light. He focused on what work didn't get done, what the new issue of the week was, or who wasn't doing his job. His negative attitude about the work, people, and purpose of the project sapped people's energy, enthusiasm, and passion. It was a self-fulfilling prophecy: The project failed because the project manager willed it to fail.

This one's simple. A glass-is-half-empty manager will be a horrible motivator and will sap a team's energy. This doesn't mean that you have to be a shiny-happy person all the time, but that a manager has to truly believe in what he or she is doing and needs to positively motivate the team to get there.

Cowardice

Imagine this: a manager who, when pressed on a budget or schedule overrun, blames team members, stakeholders, and anyone else who could possibly have contributed to his nonperformance. It's much easier to play the blame game and implicate others because everything didn't go as planned.

> *A leader needs to be the first to admit his or her mistakes and learn from them.*

It's perfectly okay to be self-critical and aware of your own weaknesses and mistakes. For a leader to truly continue to grow in her leadership capabilities, she needs to be the first to admit her mistakes and learn from them as opposed to being the last to admit them.

Untrustworthiness

Simply put, managers who don't display the necessary skills, show wisdom in their decisions, or demonstrate integrity won't be trusted. For the team to truly have trust in their leader, they need to believe that the manager has the skills to manage the team, the wisdom to make sound business decisions, and the integrity to put the team's interests ahead of his or her own. Take away any one of these attributes, and it's just a matter of time before the manager gets voted off the island.

To truly lead and inspire people, you have to demonstrate attributes that will cause people to want to follow you. Determine if you have any of the seven barriers, and put a plan in place to break down the barrier and get people to want to follow you.

TRUTH 54

CREDIBILITY HUMPS GET SMOOTHED THROUGH LEARNING

Frank was a young consultant who was given a project management assignment to help a client install a financial management computer system. Upon arriving at the client's office, Frank would hear comments like "I've got shoes older than you" and "You just don't understand our business." Frank tried to develop project plans, conduct status meetings, and assign people to tasks. A few people took his direction, but most of the client's personnel just ignored him. The project eventually got so far behind schedule that Frank was removed from the project and another project manager was brought in to complete it. Frank was perplexed; he knew how to manage projects and felt that he was doing the right things. The problem? Frank never established the credibility he needed to earn the client's respect.

As a young consultant I was frequently put into situations with new clients where there was some aspect of their business I didn't know. Whether it was a new functional area, a new technology, or a new industry, there was always something I had to learn to be able to get up to speed quickly and establish credibility with the client. The point is that once I got over the credibility hump, I earned the right for the client to accept input and be open to my influence. Until that happened, my ability to get my point across and influence the client was limited at best.

I've used the following basic strategies to help me get over the credibility hump:

- **Read up about the organizations you're not as familiar with.** When managing a team with members representing multiple organizations or interests, ensure that you have at least a basic understanding of the organization, its direction statement, and its challenges. The more you know about the organizations represented in your team, the better you can ensure that the direction in which you are heading is best not only for the overall organization but for each of the represented organizations.

- **Interview people who can help you learn.** When working with a new organization, take some time to talk to the people who either work in the organization or who understand it well. In addition to understanding their challenges, you'll also gain some insight into the organization's personalities and internal politics.

- **Learn about current trends or issues facing the industry.** Do some research. If you're working with a PTA organization, what are some of their major challenges in raising funds or determining how funds get allocated? Go to the library or get on the Internet and learn about some of the key industry issues that face the organization you're working with. Aside from being more effective in working with the organization, you'll potentially bring some fresh insight to their current problems.

- **Walk in their shoes.** Take on some of the tasks that will help you better learn about your organization. Working with an organization that provides customer support? Spend a day on the phones. Helping an organization redesign its shipping processes? Spend a day in the warehouse picking, packing, and shipping orders. You'll not only learn firsthand about some of their issues, but you'll also earn brownie points for your willingness to learn by doing, as opposed to learning by observing.

> *If you're helping an organization redesign its shipping processes, spend a day in the warehouse.*

- **Get a coach.** When working with a new organization, find someone in that organization who can help coach you on organization processes, personalities, and politics. For the cost of a soft drink or lunch, I have learned volumes about how an organization functions and how I can be more effective. Find a good coach and learn from him or her.

Effectively influencing others who don't work for you means establishing credibility with them quickly and getting over the "he or she doesn't get it" curve as fast as you can.

Get over the hump by walking in their shoes, learning about their organization, finding a coach, and understanding the industry, and you'll establish the credibility you need to get your point across.

TRUTH 55

BEING PARTIAL BREEDS DISTRUST

A number of years back I was assigned to a cross-organizational team that had an objective to figure out how office space would be allocated across all the organizations. Six organizations were represented on the team, and the team leader was also a representative of one of the organizations. Each representative needed to ensure that his or her organization's office space needs were met, but at the same time play fairly with the other representatives. The team leader called the first meeting. We all got in the room and started looking at the available space and how it would be allocated. It became very clear very quickly that the team leader would ensure that her organization's needs were met and that she would use her position as team leader to make it happen. Immediately, distrust formed on the team, and we

The team leader used her position to ensure her organization's needs, creating distrust on the team.

got very little done. The team ultimately disbanded without having completed its objective. The root cause of our failure as a team was a team leader who wasn't impartial.

Leading cross-organizational teams mandates that the team leader show allegiance to the team's direction statement over and above any personal or organizational desires. Showing preference to any team member or organization ensures distrust and strife among the team. Impartiality is a crucial component of success for the team.

The best impartial team leaders do the following to keep a level playing field:

- **Learn about organizations you're not as familiar with.** When managing a team with members representing multiple organizations or interests, ensure that you have at least a basic understanding of the organization, its direction statement, and its challenges. The more you know about the organizations represented on your team, the better you can ensure that the direction in which you are heading is best not only for the overall organization but for each of the represented organizations.

- **Show no bias in work assignments.** When assigning tasks, ensure that the people best qualified to complete the tasks are appropriately assigned. Showing consistent favoritism or bias toward some team members and giving them the more "cushy" tasks, while others get the "grungy" tasks, will contribute to your being labeled as a partial leader and will damage your credibility with the team. Spread the grungy tasks around, even if it means you do a grungy task.

- **Show equality when holding team members accountable for their work.** When reviewing progress on tasks, be consistent in your treatment of the team members who complete tasks on time as well as those who do not meet deadlines. Whether it's praise of a job well done or questioning a job not yet done, do so equally among the team members.

- **Resolve disputes equitably.** This is particularly important if you have a personal stake in the dispute. The team needs to see that you are governed by sound, reasonable decision criteria and that you will enforce a decision even if it doesn't meet your personal stake. Driving a decision that shows that your personal interests are secondary to the team's interests speaks volumes about your ability to be an impartial leader.

- **Be cautious about socializing too much with only part of the team.** It's great to get to know the team on a social basis, but excessive socializing with only part of the team can get you labeled as someone who plays favorites. By all means, have a milkshake with the team; just make sure you're fair about how you spend your social time and who you spend it with.

- **Recognize and reward team members fairly.** Just as the leader holds all team members equally accountable, he or she needs to recognize and reward noteworthy performance fairly across the team. Don't worry about having to change your rewards system just because you have a cross-organizational team; by all means, use whatever rewards system seems to work for you and your organization. Just remember to include those employees who are outside your organization but are working on your team.

Leading a cross-organizational team requires you to demonstrate your impartiality to the team. Assign tasks fairly, hold everyone equally accountable, praise equitably, and resolve disputes with the team's overall interests in mind. By all means, socialize with the team; just don't play favorites. Your demonstrated impartiality will help the team see you as someone worth following.

PART XIII

THE TRUTH ABOUT COMMUNICATING GLOBALLY

TRUTH 56

IT'S NOT ALL ABOUT THE IVORY TOWER

One of my jobs at Microsoft was running the Corporate Procurement Group. This group was responsible for managing and influencing several billion dollars in purchases, ranging from personal computers to marketing materials to outsourced services. My organization had about 30 procurement managers who resided at headquarters and worked with various organizations around Microsoft to help get better value for our purchases. To better expand our global influence, we started working with procurement organizations in Microsoft subsidiaries around the world to understand their purchases and to find areas where we could partner. What we learned was more than what we had anticipated—not necessarily about their purchases, but about how they worked and the significance of urgency versus importance in their jobs. For example, in some of the smaller subsidiaries, the person responsible for procurement was also responsible for facilities management—meaning that if the toilets didn't flush, it was his responsibility to get them fixed. Given the choice between working on a global procurement contract and getting the toilets fixed, he would tend to the toilets first (rightly so).

Given the choice between working on a global procurement contract and getting the toilets fixed, he chose the toilets.

Getting this exposure to the subsidiaries taught me a very important lesson about working with organizations outside headquarters: It's not all about the ivory tower.

As I discussed in Truth 2, understanding communication expectations is very important to establishing an effective transfer of information between you and your colleague. When it comes to communicating across organizations or cultures, understanding what other people do, what their priorities are, and what is important to them also contributes to getting your point across effectively. Now, I'm not saying that if you're going to have a conversation with someone you need to research his job and priorities. I am referring to situations where you will be communicating with a colleague on a regular basis in order to get something done together.

When faced with regular communication with a colleague in another organization or culture, pave the way using some of these techniques:

- **Understand your colleague's job responsibilities.** Just as in the preceding example, you may have a colleague who has a job title similar to yours but could have a radically different set of responsibilities. Assume little about job titles; get an understanding from your colleague of what she is responsible for.

- **Understand your colleague's priorities.** In addition to responsibilities, understand your colleague's relative priorities. The fact that she has three primary responsibilities doesn't mean that she spends equal time on each or that the priorities don't change. Understanding her priorities will help set your expectations for when she can respond to you and when she can't.

- **Tailor your communication to what is important to your colleague.** Communicating with your colleague is great, but she may not have the same degree of interest or need for the things you see as important in your job. Understanding what is important to her will help ensure that your communication is more targeted and that your colleague will read what you send her.

Just because you have the same job title and are part of the same organization doesn't mean you do the same things. Take time to understand what your colleague does and what she considers important. Target your communications to meet her needs. Doing so will better ensure that your colleague gets the information that is most important to her and ensures that you aren't wasting your time creating irrelevant information.

TRUTH 57

You Have to Talk to Them, Even if It's After Hours

In Truth 56 I described my job at Microsoft managing Corporate Procurement. In this job I had two peers: a European manager and an Asia Pacific manager. The European manager was based in London, and the Asia Pacific manager was based in Japan. To better ensure that the various procurement organizations worked well together, I realized that I needed to focus on building a relationship with each of my peers. We decided to put a simple communications plan in place to help the relationship-building.

I established a pattern of regular biweekly phone calls, which I made with each of my peers. We agreed up front to block out the time on our calendars regardless of our agendas and to take only the amount of time necessary. I scheduled my calls at 8 a.m. with my European peer and at 4 p.m. with my Asia Pacific peer to ensure that we would be doing the calls during work hours for both of us. Sometimes the calls had some important issues and decisions that we needed to discuss, and other times the issues weren't as important. Sometimes we socialized during the calls, and sometimes not. Each call was important, though, in that it helped build trust in the relationship and strengthen our sense of teaming with each other. A significant part of our organizations working well together was the fact that our respective leadership took the time to get to know each other and develop a personal relationship.

In today's world of the Internet and e-mail, it is very easy for us to want to utilize the efficiency that technology has to offer in how we communicate. Don't get me wrong; I'm not advocating bringing back the pony express as a means of communication. I love technology and use e-mail and the Internet every day. I do think that at times, particularly when communicating across cultures or time zones, you need to get on the phone and talk. Talking real-time to a colleague provides an additional dimension to your interaction that e-mail doesn't. Aside from being less time-consuming than e-mail, talking on the phone better facilitates building a relationship with your colleague. Hearing a person's voice makes a message more personal and allows you to better understand emotions like frustration, happiness, fear, and sadness.

I've found that by getting on the phone and talking with a colleague, I can get a much better appreciation of his or her business challenges, empathize with his or her situation, and establish trust in our relationship.

> *Hearing a person's voice makes a message more personal and allows you to better understand his or her emotions.*

If you have a cross-cultural colleague you need to build a relationship with, put a few techniques to work to help you both get your point across more effectively:

- **Schedule regular phone discussions.** Agree with your colleague on how often you'll talk, who will call whom, and how structured or unstructured the phone calls will be. Regularly scheduled discussions will help set expectations for both you and your colleague on when you will talk as well as enable you to "save up" agenda items for your next phone discussion.

- **Alternate who gets up early or stays at work late.** If you're working in different time zones and are unable to schedule discussions during business hours for both of you, alternate who gets in extra early or stays late. Aside from showing a degree of courtesy to your colleague, this also shows a commitment to the relationship, because you're willing to work outside normal business hours to talk with your colleague.

- **Be prepared.** Spend some time thinking about the items you want to discuss, get an idea of how long each will take, and send your discussion items to your colleague ahead of time. I'm not suggesting that your phone discussion be too rigid or structured. Just make an effort to use both your and your colleague's time well by preparing up front.

Getting your point across effectively to a colleague from another time zone, country, or culture means you need to take some time to talk real-time. Get him or her on the phone to discuss issues, talk about projects, or ask about family. Talking together helps you put a personality behind the words and better paves the way to a more effective relationship between the two of you.

TRUTH 58

FACE-TO-FACE PAVES THE COMMUNICATION HIGHWAY

Several years back I made a trip to Japan for a finance conference. The conference went very well. Some great ideas were exchanged, the attendees were very active and interested, and we all learned some outstanding things about each other's organizations. All in all it was a very successful conference. The most memorable part, though, was a dinner I enjoyed with a colleague.

My colleague, Ikawa, took me to an exclusive Japanese (we were in Japan, after all) restaurant high atop a Tokyo skyscraper. I vowed to Ikawa that I would eat anything he ate. He gave me an approving nod and began ordering for us. The first serving came. It was a square of tofu with a pink gelatinous glop of goo on top. I asked, "Ikawa, what is this?" He replied, "Let's see, how do you say in English... oh yes, pickled fish stomach!" Then he ate it in two bites. I looked at my dish, remembered my pledge, and ate it in one bite, fearing that if I hated the first bite I wouldn't be able to stomach (no pun intended) the second bite. It wasn't that bad, but I can't say I'd eat a whole bowl of it. The second course was a 6-inch long whole smoked fish. I asked Ikawa how to eat the fish; he picked it up whole, bit right into the middle, and left only bones behind. Yeesh. So I did the same, realizing only after I had taken a bite that the organs were still in the fish, which was now in my mouth. In addition to the meat, I got to experience all the organs. Fortunately, Ikawa didn't eat the head, because I think I would have needed to draw the line there. The rest of the dinner was all more familiar food, but we laughed a lot about my cultural indoctrination to Japanese dining for years thereafter.

Taking time to work, laugh, and socialize face-to-face with colleagues from other cultures is an outstanding means to build the relationships you need to get things done. Whether you are trying to educate, influence, or collaborate, doing so face-to-face will help you not only communicate more effectively but also build relationships with colleagues along the way. As discussed in Truth 57, strong trusting and collaborative relationships with your colleagues are essential to building an effective communications pipeline that will permit a free and easy flow of information between you.

> *Taking time to work, laugh, and socialize face-to-face with colleagues helps you build relationships.*

Before you jump on a plane to meet with colleagues, consider doing the following:

- ■ **Piggyback on another meeting.** When going to Europe and Asia, I would schedule my visits around some other event where people from that region would already be getting together. You'll be more efficient by meeting with multiple colleagues in a single location, and you'll be able to participate in a meeting already being held.

- **Use the opportunity to educate and be educated.** Use your visit to educate people about your respective organizations, discuss high-profile initiatives, and explore ways to better partner together. The more you can learn about each other and understand each other's organizations, the more you can better help each other work more effectively.

- **Pack your time full of meetings.** Sleep when you get home. Fill your time with meeting colleagues, customers, suppliers, partners, or anyone else who can potentially impact your organization. Spend plenty of time interacting and socializing, and save the head-down work for the plane ride.

- **Experience their culture socially.** I've found that colleagues from other cultures love to entertain you with activities native to their culture. I've built some of my best relationships while talking, laughing, and eating things I didn't recognize. Embrace their culture, be a part of it, and laugh at yourself along the way.

- **Travel in moderation.** I had one colleague who used to travel between Seattle and Paris at least twice a month and stay a week at a time. Travel is not only time-consuming and taxing on the body and mind; it is also expensive. Travel when you need to; stay at home when you don't.

■ **Keep your moral and ethical antenna up.** Doing the right thing is the same in Peoria as it is in Prague. In some cultures, activities such as taking and offering bribes or turning a blind eye to cheating are tolerated behaviors. That doesn't mean, though, that you have to participate. Don't compromise your moral and ethical standards just because others around you are engaging in unscrupulous behavior. You may get some quizzical looks, but you'll go to bed at night knowing you are conducting business without compromising your standards of ethics. And your credibility with colleagues will skyrocket.

Meeting, communicating, and socializing with colleagues from another culture is a great way to build relationships and pave the way to getting your point across. When you do travel, make the most out of your visit and socialize with your hosts. Just make sure you have a good reason to travel and that the trip makes business and financial sense.

TRUTH 59

JUST BECAUSE THEY CAN SPEAK YOUR NATIVE TONGUE DOESN'T MEAN THEY UNDERSTAND EVERYTHING YOU SAY

Some years back I gave a presentation to a group of Japanese colleagues who spoke English relatively well. I launched into the presentation, not really thinking much about the fact that English was their second language. I had a lot of very rich content in the presentation and explained some of the intricacies of my topic in great detail. I used my regular attempts at humor that would kill a room in the U.S. (well, maybe not kill a room), but in Japan you could hear crickets chirping. At the end of my presentation my colleagues spoke in Japanese to each other for about 5 minutes while I stood there wondering what was happening. After their 5-minute discussion, the leader in the room turned to me and said, "This was good; thank you," and then they left. Now, I don't know that much Japanese, but I *do* know that it doesn't take 5 minutes to say "This was good." Afterward, one of my colleagues gave me the scoop. "They liked you and all, but they couldn't understand you," he said. "You used too many unfamiliar terms, and you spoke too quickly for many of them to follow. Their long discussion afterward consisted of their asking each other what some of the terminology meant and what you were trying to communicate. They finally figured it out by talking among themselves." So went my first foray into communicating with others who don't share a complete command of my native tongue.

"They liked you and all, but they couldn't understand you," he said.

In our global society, being able to communicate with others who do not share your native tongue will continue to grow as a mandatory skill for business professionals. While English has largely emerged as the de facto standard for communication, skills can vary widely among and within cultures. Understanding ahead of time the proficiency level of the organization you will be communicating with can help you close the language gap and prevent misunderstandings or confusion in your communication.

Think about the following the next time you will communicate with a group that has a different native tongue than yours:

- **Speak and write in simple terms.** Stick with basic one- or two-syllable words that get your point across simply and easily. Multisyllabic prose is great for those of your own language but will confuse the dickens out of someone who knows only the basics of your language. Keep it simple.

- **Use visuals or videos to convey your point.** A picture is worth a thousand words, particularly when you're communicating with colleagues who don't speak your native tongue. Use visuals or videos to get your point across, particularly if the visual or video is in their native tongue.

- **Watch your jargon.** Be careful with slang and jargon that might confuse those with a different native tongue. Using phrases like "That's cool" or "You're the bomb" would certainly result in some quizzical looks from those who know only the basics of your language. Use plain language that can be easily translated in someone's mind.

- **Use handouts.** If you're doing a presentation or speech, try to put at least the major points in handouts that your colleagues can look at and translate. By using handouts, you give those who don't translate quickly an opportunity to digest the material at their own speed. Another idea is to provide handouts in both languages to eliminate translation stress.

- **Speak slowly and clearly.** It sounds basic, but speak clearly, don't mumble, and pronounce slowly. Speaking slowly doesn't mean you should also speak more loudly, though. Speaking louder won't help them translate any better and may make your colleagues wonder why you are shouting.

- **Let them discuss in their native language.** If you see a conversation happening among your colleagues and they are fumbling, call a "time-out" and let them speak in their own language for a few minutes. After they're done, ask one of them to summarize for you if you couldn't follow the conversation. This could be a bit uncomfortable for you, but it might be essential to helping your colleagues express themselves with each other.

- **Find out about the colleague's language level.** Ask someone who knows the organization about the language level, and gauge your communication appropriately. For organizations that are very comfortable with your native tongue, you don't need to be as concerned as you would with those who are less comfortable with your language. Ask ahead of time, and gauge your communication appropriately.

- **Don't try to convey too many points in a single conversation.** Create focus in your discussion by having a single objective and sticking to that objective. If you combine topics in a single conversation or meeting, your colleagues not only have to translate the language, they also have to keep track of what topic is being discussed. Give your meeting a singular objective, or break a larger meeting into smaller meetings to ensure that focus is maintained.

Conversing with colleagues who have different native tongues can be frustrating and confusing. When you compound the confusion with slang, ten-dollar words, and fast speech, the communication can become ineffective. Respect the fact that others don't share your language at the same level, and speak in accessible terms, speak clearly, and don't use jargon. Use handouts when you can, preferably in their language. Don't make getting your point across even tougher than it needs to be by forgetting they don't speak your native tongue well.

REFERENCES

1. Source: www.phrases.org.uk

2. Source: www.wordherders.net

3. Source: www.nsaspeaker.org

4. Source: www.socialanxietyassist.com.au

5. Source: Pacelli, Lonnie, *The Project Management Advisor*, Prentice Hall, August 2004

6. If you would like a copy of this status report template go to www.projectmanagementadvisor.com and find the status report under "templates".

7. Source: www.3m.com

8. Source: www.jobmonkey.com

9. Peters, Thomas J. and Robert H. Waterman. *In Search of Excellence*, HarperCollins Publishers, Inc., 1982.

The Truth About Managing Your Career
...and Nothing But the Truth
BY KAREN OTAZO

This is your concise, fast-paced guide to achieving maximum career success. Drawing on her work with 2,000+ leaders and business professionals, and her analysis of hundreds of secret feedback reports, Dr. Otazo identifies 60 crucial career challenges—and winning solutions! Here are breakthrough techniques for succeeding at a new job...working more smoothly with bosses and colleagues...building a high-performance personal network...managing your workload...deciding who to trust (and distrust)... handling enemies and overcoming setbacks... recognizing when to move on...getting noticed, getting ahead, getting to the top!

ISBN 0131873369, © 2006, 272 pp., $18.99

PUBLISHING IN 2007

The Truth About Being an Effective Leader
...and Nothing But the Truth
BY KAREN OTAZO

Leadership isn't just another step in your career; it's a leap across the great divide. In this book, you'll be learning from the real-life challenges and successes of those who have made the leap. For more than two decades Dr. Otazo has worked with hundreds of leaders worldwide. Her approach gives you necessary guidance to get through the hard work and sticky situations in 52 short, to-the-point chapters that you can shuffle like a deck of cards and use as you need them. You'll learn to steer past the pitfalls and through each challenge as you make the transition to becoming the most effective leader possible.

ISBN 0131873385, © 2007, 208 pp., $18.99

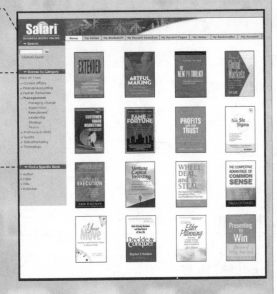